THE TANK COMMANDER

Pocket Manual 1939–1945

Edited by R. Sheppard

POOLOFLONDON

Ruth Sheppard read Ancient and Modern history at St John's College, Oxford and has an interest in all periods of history. Ruth has worked for many years in military publishing for leading companies such as Casemate and Osprey, and has authored and compiled a number of books including *Empires Collide: The French Indian War 1754–68, Extraordinary Heroes: Amazing Stories of Victoria Cross and George Cross Recipients* and *Alexander the Great at War.*

This edition published in Great Britain in 2016 by
The Pool of London Press
A Division of Casemate Publishers
10 Hythe Bridge Street
Oxford OX1 2EW, UK
and
1950 Lawrence Road, Havertown, PA 19083 USA

Compilation, Introduction and chapter introductory texts by Ruth Sheppard
© Pool of London Press 2016

A CIP record for this book is available from the British Library

Images on pages 138 and 147 reproduced courtesy of The National Archives.
All material by Reginald James Spittles reproduced courtesy of the Tank Museum, Bovington

ISBN (hardback) 978-1-910860-16-8

Interior designed by BoundUnbound Media.
Printed in the Czech Republic

Publisher's Note

This compilation contains material of historic interest. The techniques described herein must be considered in the context of their original publication or issue and the publishers exclude liability arising from reliance on the information provided to the fullest extent of the law.

References to material not included from the original in the selected extract have been excluded to avoid confusion. In certain cases superfluous text has been excluded or is missing from the original.

The Pool of London Press is committed to respecting the intellectual property rights of others. We have therefore taken all reasonable efforts to ensure that the reproduction of all text is done with the full consent of copyright holders. If you are aware of any unintentional omissions, please contact the company so that any necessary corrections can be made for future editions of this book.

To find out more please visit www.pooloflondon.com and to receive regular email updates on forthcoming Pool of London titles, email info@pooloflondon.com with Pool of London Updates in the subject field. www.pooloflondon.com

For a complete list of Pool of London Press and Casemate titles, please contact:

CASEMATE PUBLISHERS (UK); Telephone (01865) 241249; Email: casemate-uk@casematepublishers.co.uk
www.casematepublishers.co.uk

CASEMATE PUBLISHERS (US) Telephone (610) 853-9131; Email: casemate@casematepublishing.com
www.casematepublishing.com

Contents

The Pool of London Press is a new publisher inspired by the rich history and resonance of the stretch of the River Thames from London Bridge downriver to Greenwich. The Press is dedicated to the specialist fields of naval, maritime, military and exploration history in its many forms. The Press produces beautifully designed, commercial, non-fiction volumes and digital products of outstanding quality for a dedicated readership featuring strong narratives, magnificent illustrations and the finest photography. Recent titles include:

THE LAST BIG GUN
At War & At Sea with HMS *Belfast*
Brian Lavery
£25.00 • Hardback • 376 pages • ISBN: 978-1-910860-01-4

THE COLD WAR SPY POCKET MANUAL
The Official Field-manuals for Spycraft, Espionage and Counter-intelligence
Edited and compiled by Philip Parker
£8.99 • Hardback • 160 pages • ISBN: 978-1-910860-02-1

THE MAPMAKERS' WORLD
A Cultural History of the European World Map
Marjo T. Nurminen
£50.00 • Hardback • 360 pages • ISBN: 978-1-910860-00-7

POOLOFLONDON

www.pooloflondon.com

Introduction

Tanks first lumbered into history and into the public imagination at Flers–Courcelette, during the Somme Offensive, in September 1916. The slow and alien-looking British Mark I tanks provoked awe and terror as they rolled across no man's land, and quickly became the hot topic for the newspapers of the day. The French deployed their first tanks in the spring of 1917, and developed the first practical light tank, the revolutionary Renault FT, which saw service with the French and the American Expeditionary Force. In response the Germans managed to develop and deploy a small number of tanks, and the first tank against tank battle came in 1918. But even as designs were improved and production increased so that tanks could be deployed en masse, they were just too slow and unreliable to break the stalemate on the Western Front.

In the years after Versailles, the combatant nations of the First World War began to evaluate their experiences so that they could plan for future conflicts. While to some it seemed clear that tanks would be instrumental in modern warfare, others did not recognise the promise of armoured fighting vehicles or mechanisation. Even as the technology made huge strides, some traditionalists dismissed tanks as unreliable and unnecessary. Opinion was divided about the role of tanks: should they be used solely to support infantry, should they act independently, in mechanised formations, or should the armies of the future be entirely mechanised? There was no one answer, and by the late 1930s, years of research, development, and testing had resulted in a wide variety of armoured doctrines, with tanks developed, formations organised and crews trained to match the chosen strategy. With few opportunities in which to prove or disprove these theories in combat, the controversies continued until well into the Second World War.

Though different hardware, strategy, political doctrine, and theatres of war shaped the experience of individual tank crewmen and tank commanders during the war, there were features common to the experience of most

Second World War tankers. Competent tank men embodied a unique combination of mechanical expertise, marksmanship, and the flexibility to adapt to the new fighting machine. Because of this, they were often young, and many came from farming or industrial backgrounds, which meant they were used to working with large machinery. Some men came to the tanks from cavalry units, though only those able to adapt would survive. The often quite egalitarian atmosphere inside a tank was influenced by this intake. Uniquely among the armies of the Second World War, some Soviet tank crews included women, mainly as drivers.

Living and working in a claustrophobic metal box, the crew would become close-knit. Depending on each other's skills and nerve even more than infantrymen, camaraderie was bound to develop. The demands of life in a tank were exhausting, and the men would have to work together and look after each other if they were to survive. Special care would be taken of the driver because driving a tank was so physically exhausting. As he was also responsible for maintaining the engine, it was in everyone's interest that he be allowed to sleep whenever possible; his comrades might well take it in turns to keep up a constant chatter to keep him awake on long marches. Watching for the enemy for long periods, especially through vision blocks or periscopes, the constant bone-shaking motion of a moving tank, and the continual need for maintenance when the tank was stopped all meant a tanker could fall asleep anywhere – as any number of wartime photos attest.

All tankers lived in fear of their tank 'brewing up', when a tank sustained damage which resulted in the ignition of the fuel and ammunition. Some tanks were more prone to catching fire than others, but the danger was always present, and the men knew how difficult it was to bale out of an burning tank through the hatches in time – often under enemy machine-gun fire. Most tankers would at one time or another have been forced to watch helplessly as another tank burned with its crew trapped inside.

The tank commander was responsible for his men and the tank. Usually a junior officer or NCO, the lives of a crew depended on the commander's ability, skill, and courage – although his ability would be irrelevant if his crew weren't capable. He was responsible for getting his crew to safety if the tank was knocked out, and he would write to their family if they were killed. High in the moving, jolting turret a commander had to juggle a huge range of responsibilities: navigating, reading the ground and observing for the enemy, spotting targets and directing fire, while maintaining contact with his crew and other tanks on different wavelengths on his wireless (radio) set.

An experienced commander would thoroughly understand all the roles of his crew – he would often have been trained in one or more of them. Some German commanders were accomplished gunners or drivers, though the German tank ace Otto Carius was previously a loader, the most junior role in a tank crew. Commanders were selected on their leadership and their ability to understand the tactical situation, make fast decisions, and communicate them to their crew. He had to combine the technical and tactical aspects of tank warfare, understanding what his unit was trying to achieve, and how his tank could contribute to that. Speed was always of the essence.

Finally, good tank commanders possibly had to have a greater reserve of courage than other soldiers; they left the protection of the tank in order to recce, and many defied their training and kept the cupola hatch open even as they advanced into battle, so they could better observe the battlefield. A British report noted that in North Africa: 'Once again too high a proportion of tank commanders became casualties from small arms fire while observing their own fire with tanks opened up; in one brigade alone six tank commanders were killed and eight wounded in this way.' (*Notes from Theatres of War* 14) As in all combat, there was a fine line between bravery and foolhardiness: a commander who demonstrated the latter might get a medal, or might get his crew killed.

After campaigning in Italy in 1943, the commanding officer of 1st Royal Tank Regiment produced a document of 'Lessons'. The first section stressed the importance of good leadership to enable armoured forces to be successful in this theatre:

> If decisions are to be obtained and excessive casualties avoided with tanks in this type of country, the very highest degree of leadership is required, especially in troop commanders. The average range of vision was 50 yards, the average range at which tanks were knocked out 80 yards. Decisions must be made instantly; to hesitate spells death. Initiative and resource in carrying out recces on foot, skill in choosing a line across country and keeping direction are essential qualities. It is only too easy as soon as a gun opens fire, or a tank is knocked out, to say that you can't get on and yell for the infantry. With the present organisation, equipment and training of infantry that entails a delay of hours before any further movement occurs, and all hope of surprise is lost. The determination and initiative of tank and troop commanders to find and destroy the enemy

7

and continue the advance alone maintains the impetus of armoured movement. If the speed of the advance is to be the speed of the man on foot, there is no justification for an Armoured Division. The qualities required are (a) speed of sight, thought and action. This is innate and no amount of training will produce it. Officers and NCOs may be keen, courageous, determined, hard working and intelligent, but until they have these qualities of speed, they are useless in tanks. Age dulls speed and the younger the better. ... The standard required of all commanders down to tank commanders is higher than in any other branch of the service. Any commander who does not reach the required standard is not only useless, but quickly demoralizes the crews of his own and other tanks.

This book brings together some of the original training manuals, documents and reports which were either prepared for tank commanders and crews to read, or would have framed their training or provided the context for their orders. The reports of action would have informed their approach to future actions. Of course these manuals were 'neat and orderly' compared to the reality of war, and training varied tremendously between countries, units, and at different times of the war. Some training was thorough and practical, while other training was hopelessly out of step with the situation on the ground, a fact often obvious to the trainees. While this short book can give only a glimpse into the world of the tank commander, the concluding battle accounts provide a flavour of how tank commanders implemented their training, used their initiative, and got the job done.

CHAPTER 1: CREW TRAINING

W hile tank crew training varied tremendously according to the country, the type of unit, and its role, all tankers would have learnt the same basics. The ideal outcome was a cohesive, trained crew. British training tended to emphasise flexibility, with crews trained to some level in all roles – driver, loader, operator, gunner – before specialising in one role, though their level of expertise in any aspect inevitably varied due to the available time for training. Certain of these roles would be combined in the tanks with smaller crews. German tank men were initially trained in their particular role, and only later might be trained for a second position. US crews tended to be very well trained because many units were formed in 1942 and didn't enter combat for two years, by which time tankers had trained for several roles.

All men would be trained in tank and weapon maintenance, and correct stowage of equipment in the tank. While this may have seemed trivial in training, especially when crews might not even have had access to a tank, let alone their full complement of equipment, in fact it could mean the difference between life and death: 'Tanks must not be filled with miscellaneous kit – greatcoats, extra blankets, private stores etc. It has been found that, when loading tables are not strictly adhered to, doors become obstructed and may not readily open in emergency, with the result that troops are trapped inside.' (*Notes from Theatres of War* 13)

Of course when the pressure to send units or replacements to the front increased, the training period might be severely curtailed. The full German training programme was maintained well into the war, though it was eventually much abbreviated as armoured units were urgently needed at the front. Replacements who had been rushed through training could cause problems for the whole crew, as Bert Rendell, a sergeant tank commander in 1st Royal Tank Regiment, recalled: 'In the Mk VI the operator used a radio and laid the gun. You have to be careful when you talk about driver-operators; they may have had a fortnight's training to drive a tank, then they find out he's not too good at driving, so he's sent to learn to be a radio-operator. He's not bad at that so he's sent to the regiment as driver-operator but he can't really drive a tank'.

The value of a well-trained tank crew was immense, as noted in a British report on the 1942 fighting in the Western Desert and Cyrenaica: 'As Rommel has shown by his conduct of successive withdrawals, the most important and least easily replaceable part of a mechanized army are the highly trained technicians and tank crews, rather than the tanks themselves. After the breakthrough at El Alamein the Axis commanders abandoned many of their tanks, but saved the crews by loading them into lorries and sending them back, leaving infantry to form the backbone of the rearguards. These crews were therefore the prize and until they were either killed or captured, the destruction of the Africa Korps could not be regarded as complete.' (*Notes from Theatres of War* 14)

The number of men in a crew varied according to the size of tank and the number of weapons it mounted, with the American M3 medium tank crew numbering seven, but this British official training manual of 1941 clearly explains the various roles and tasks of a four- or five-man cruiser tank crew.

Military Training Pamphlet No. 51: Troop Training for Cruiser Tank Troops

Chapter 1: THE ORGANISATION AND TRAINING OF A CRUISER TANK CREW

Organisation

The crew of a cruiser tank consists of a commander, a gunner, a driver, a loader, and, in some marks of cruiser tank, a forward gunner.

They are responsible for the following:—

1. The commander.
    i.   The efficiency of the tank and the training and welfare of the crew.
    ii. The supervision of the duties of the other members of the crew.
    iii. The tactical handling of the tank.
    iv. The stowage of the tank.
2. The gunner.
    i.   The efficiency and maintenance of the main turret weapons, spares and tools.
    ii. The maintenance of the turret traversing gear.

3. The driver.
    i.   The general mechanical efficiency of the tank.
    ii. The maintenance and stowage of the driver's spares and tools.
4. The loader.
    i.   The condition and stowage of the ammunition for the main turret weapons.
    ii. The maintenance and tuning of the wireless set.
5. The forward gunner (in certain marks of cruiser tanks).
    i.   The efficiency and maintenance of the subsidiary turret weapon.
    ii. The condition and stowage of the ammunition for the subsidiary turret weapon.
    iii. The maintenance of the subsidiary turret traversing gear.

Objects

The object of crew training is to produce a team.

While each member of a crew must be master of his own particular function, all must be interchangeable.

The purpose of crew training, therefore, is to ensure that every member:—

    Is able to drive and maintain the tank.

    Is master of the tank's weapons.

    Is able to use (including tuning in) the wireless, and has a knowledge of signal codes.

    Is a good map reader.

    Is able to cook on the tank cooking set.

    Has a knowledge of first-aid.

    Has a thorough knowledge of the tactics of his own units.

    Is able to handle the Bren gun and fight dismounted should his tank become a casualty.

The crew must be able to work together in the cramped conditions inside a tank with the minimum direction from the tank commander.

Driving

1. The driver must drive in such as a way as to:—

    Make the fullest use of ground and cover to escape observation. Skylines must be avoided; full advantage must be taken of shadows.

    Assist the gunner to apply fire to the best advantage.

Achieve the most rapid and economical progress, saving petrol and avoiding unnecessary jostling to the crew and the machine.

Facilitate observation by the tank commander.

2. All the above must be achieved by the driver without constant orders and directions from the tank commander.

Gunnery

The gunner must be able to:—

Pick up targets quickly on brief orders. This can only be done if the gunner is constantly on the alert and anticipating targets by his own observation.

Apply self-imposed fire discipline to conserve ammunition and make full use of every round.

Correct his range after observation of first round.

Wireless

It is the loader's duty to look after the wireless set, to tune it in for use by the tank commander.

Once the set is tuned in, the loader should look after the ammunition and ensure that the guns are kept loaded and, except for periodical attention, leave the operating of the set to the tank commander.

Maintenance

The crew must be determined to keep their tank in action. Mechanical failure of the tank through an avoidable cause is a personal disgrace reflecting on every member of the crew. If their tank breaks down through accident the crew must spare no effort to repair it and rejoin the troop. Calls by the crew for assistance from the unit fitters of R.A.O.C. should only be made reluctantly as the last resort in cases where repair is entirely beyond the resources of the crew. Mechanical failures can only be avoided by thorough and continuous maintenance during periods in harbour and at halts on the line of march. Every member of the crew must have his own definite responsibility so that every part of the tank and equipment is constantly inspected and maintained.

After a day's work no tank must be left by its crew until it is mechanically fit, refuelled, replenished with ammunition and ready for action the next day.

Petrol and oil must be replenished at every opportunity during and operation.

Maintenance comes before rest.

All tank crew training would foster the cooperation and interaction needed between the men in a tank; the hours of drill not only made common tasks second nature but also bonded the men into a unit. The instruction book for the Matilda Infantry Tank Mks I–V sets out crew drill:

Crew drill

(a) General
Crew drill lays down the procedure which will be followed by the crew at all times. It includes all routine whether the tank is stationary, on the march, or in action.

The object of crew drill, the basis of which is the same for all tank crews, is to ensure that the necessary actions of the crew are most rapid and efficient.

The crew consists of 4 men who are allotted specific independent duties and are numbered as under:

No. 1: Crew commander.
No. 2: Driver-mechanic (A.F.V.).
No. 3: Gunner-operator.
No. 4: Wireless Operator (A.F.V.).

(b) "Crews Front"
Normal position of the crew dismounted. Crew will be in line 3 paces in front of the tank facing front and standing "at ease" and dressed on:

No. 1: Immediately in front of the offside track.
No. 2: On left of No. 1.
No. 3: On left of No. 2.
No. 4: On left of No. 3 and in front of nearside track.

(c) "Crews Right/Left"
Crews will form up in the same order as for "Crews Front," in line with the centre of the turret, the inside flank man 1½ paces from side of tank.

(d) "Crews Rear"
Crews will form up in same order as before, but facing the rear of the tank.

(e) "Report"
This order will be given when all crews have formed "Crews Front" on completion of "Inspect Maintenance."

Crew commanders will report to their troop commanders who in turn will report to their next senior.

(f) "Mount"

Crews will come to attention, turn about and mount in the following order.

No. 2: If not already in the driver's seat, through the driver's hood.

No. 3: Enters fighting chamber through cupola flaps and takes up his position in gunner's seat.

No. 1: Follows No. 3 and takes up his position as crew commander.

No. 4: Enters fighting chamber through turret flaps and stands on right of gun.

(g) "Dismount"

Crew will dismount in the reverse order to "Mount" and assume the "Crews Front" positions.

This US manual, *Armored Force Field Manual: Armored Force Drill*, sets out mounted drill, which enabled tank commanders to rehearse their part in battle formations, keeping a uniform speed and conforming to the movements of the unit leader.

MOUNTED DRILL

7. Purpose and Scope.—*a*. The primary purpose of mounted drill in armored force units is to facilitate control in combat.

b. Drills prescribed herein are battle formations at decreased intervals. They are adaptable to any type of armored force unit. Interpretation should be based on these general provisions and all should learn to use this manual as a guide to a simple solution of minor points which are not specifically covered in the text. Much discussion over trifles or failure to make appropriate adaptations indicates a failure to grasp the spirit of the regulations. Higher commanders should encourage subordinates to use their initiative and to make minor adjustments without calling on higher authority for interpretation.

8. The Leader.—*a*. The commander of each unit is the leader. In general, during drill, he is in front of the base element, except as otherwise shown in the figures in this manual. From this position he normally leads the unit in the direction and at the speed desired. He may, however, move his vehicle

where he can best observe and supervise his unit, leaving the guidance to a subordinate.

b. Subordinate commanders may vary the formation and speed of their units because of terrain and other conditions, but resume the original formation of the base as soon as practicable.

9. Base.—*a.* In all formations except line, wedge, and inverted wedge the base is the leading element.

b. In line, wedge, and inverted wedge formations the base is normally the center or right center element.

c. Any element may be designated as the base.

d. The base element follows its leader or conforms to his movement unless otherwise ordered. All other elements regulate and guide on the base.

e. When executing changes in formations, base elements move so as to prevent countermarching by other elements.

10. Intervals and Distances.—*a.* In close order mounted drill, intervals and distances are normally 25 yards. They may be varied to meet local conditions of terrain.

b. In extended order drill, intervals and distances are variable, usually 50 to 100 yards.

c. For mass formations see paragraph 14f.

d. For march formations see appropriate Field Manual for the unit concerned.

e. Increase or decrease of intervals or distances may be obtained at any time by the command or signal EXTEND or CLOSE.

f. Upon halting, intervals or distances are maintained unless preceded by the command or signal close. If in extended order formation, intervals and distances are decreased to those prescribed for close order drill; if in close order formation, they are decreased to 5 yards. When closed to 5 yards, no evolutions of drill are executed; close order intervals and distances are taken upon moving out unless otherwise prescribed.

11. Speed.—*a.* In close and extended order drill, the leader and base elements move at a uniform rate of speed, usually not more than 15 miles an hour.

b. Other elements, when necessary, vary their speed gradually during movements to conform with the base or to complete movements.

Figure 16.—Identifying symbols used in Figures 17 to 35.

12. Changes in Direction.—*a.* In changing the direction of a unit the leader conducts the base element in the new direction on the arc of a circle so that the pivot is able to turn on the minimum radius.

b. If the unit is in a column formation, elements in rear of the base change direction successively in the same manner and on the same ground as the base.

c. If the unit is in any formation except column, other elements regulate on the base and maintain their relative positions.

d. Changes in direction are made on a radius of not less than 15 yards.

13. Methods of Assuming Formations.—*a. Line or wedge.*—(1) These formations are gained from any column formation by a fan-shaped deployment toward either side of the base. Except in the section the next subordinate element within a unit in rear of the base moves to the left of the base and the third to the right of the base and so on alternately. These elements move by the most direct route without change of formation until they arrive near their new positions when they form line or wedge if not already in that formation. When line or wedge is to be formed in any other direction than the direction of march, the head of the column should be turned in the new direction before the deployment is ordered.

(2) In the first section the rear vehicle of the base section moves to the right; in the second section the rear vehicle moves to the left; (See fig. 17.)

b. Column.—(1) Column formations are formed from any line or wedge formation by successive movements of the next subordinate elements within a

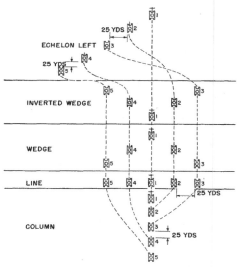

Figure 17.—Platoon formations (5 vehicles).

unit to their positions in rear of the base. Except in the section, the base is followed alternately by the next subordinate element on its left and right. These elements initiate their movement by changing their formations, if required, and moving by the most direct route to their new positions.

(2) In the section the section leader is followed by the other vehicles in its section.

c. Echelon, right (left).—(1) This formation is gained from any column formation by the next subordinate elements within a unit in rear of the base placing themselves progressively to the right (left) rear of the base. (See fig. 25.)

(2) From any line or wedge formation, echelon is gained by next subordinate elements within a unit placing themselves progressively to the right (left) rear of the base, the base being the left (right) subordinate element. This does not apply within the platoon. (See figs. 25 and 29.)

(3) Within the platoon the vehicles form in echelon in the same order as for column, moving to their positions by the most direct route. (See fig. 17.)

d. Platoons of less than five vehicles.—(1) Platoons of less than five vehicles form line, column, echelon, and wedge formation in accordance with the same principles as the platoon of five, except as shown in figures 18 and 19.

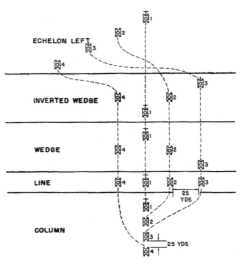

Figure 18.—Platoon formations (4 vehicles).

(2) When one section is incomplete, the platoon leader, remaining in his normal position, forms a section with the odd vehicle. (See fig. 18.)

(3) When each section has been reduced to a single vehicle, the vehicles combine to form one section. (See fig. 19.)

14. Authorized Formations and Commands for Armored Units.—The following formations and preparatory commands for same are authorized for use where applicable:

a. (1) *Line.*— All squads (vehicles) abreast of each other except the vehicles of higher commanders. (See figs. 17 and 20.)

(2) *Line of sections (platoons) (companies).*—All sections (platoons) (companies) in column and abreast. (See figs. 21, 22, and 23.)

(3) *Line of wedges.*—All companies in wedge formation and abreast.

(4) *Line of platoons (companies) in wedge.*—All platoons (companies) in platoon wedge formation and abreast. (See fig. 27.)

(5) *Line of companies, in column of sections (platoons) (platoons in wedge).*— All companies abreast and each in column of sections (platoons) (platoons in wedge). (See fig. 24.)

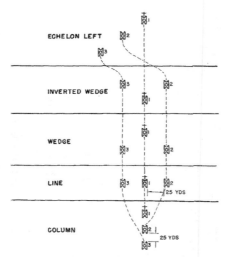

Figure 19.—Platoon formations (3 vehicles).

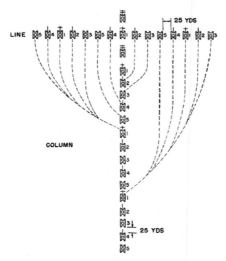

Figure 20.—Company from column to line.

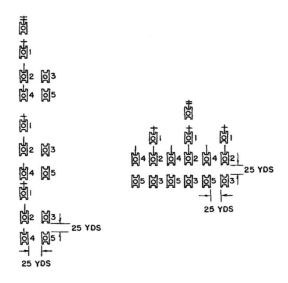

① COMPANY IN COLUMN OF SECTIONS.

② COMPANY IN LINE OF SECTIONS.

Figure 21.

b. (1) *Column.*—Each vehicle placed one behind another. (See figs. 17 and 20.)

(2) *Column of sections (platoons) (companies).*—Each section (platoon) (company) in line and placed one behind another. (See figs. 21, 25, and 26.)

(3) *Column of wedges.*—Each company in wedge formation and placed one behind another.

(4) *Column of platoons (companies) in wedge.*—Each platoon (company) in platoon wedge formation and placed one behind another. (See fig. 24.)

(5) *Column of companies, in line of sections (platoons) (platoons in wedge).*—Each company placed one behind to another and each in line of sections (platoons) (platoons in wedge). (See fig. 27.)

c. (1) *Echelon, right (left).*—Each platoon (company) displaced progressively to the right (left) rear of the base in the company (battalion) without change of formation within the platoon (company). (See figs. 22, 25, and 28.)

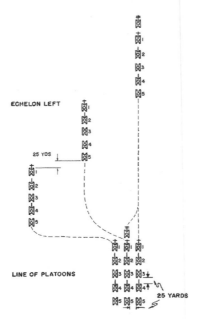

Figure 22.—Company from line of platoons to echelon left.

(2) *Platoon, echelon, right (left).*—Each vehicle displaced progressively to the right (left) rear of the base in the platoon (company). (See figs. 17 and 30.)

d. (1) *Wedge.*—Each platoon (company) displaced progressively to the left and right rear of the base in the company (battalion) without change of formation within the platoon (company). (See figs. 36 and 38.)

(2) *Platoon wedge.*—Each squad (vehicle) displaced progressively to the left and right rear of the base in the platoon (company). In assuming this formation in the company of three platoons the base platoon forms platoon wedge; the second platoon forms echelon left; and the third platoon forms echelon right. (See figs. 17, 28, and 32.)

e. (1) *Inverted wedge.*—Each platoon (company) displaced progressively forward to the left and right front of the base in the company (battalion) without change of formation within the platoon (company). (See fig. 33.)

21

Figure 23.—Line of companies.

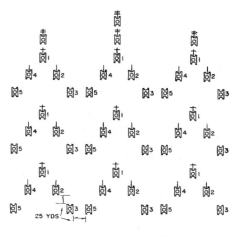

Figure 24.—Line of companies in column of platoons in wedge.

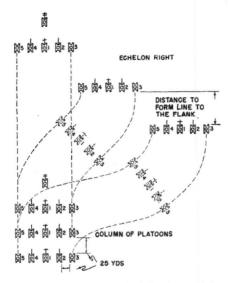

Figure 25.—Company from column of platoons to echelon right.

(2) *Platoon, inverted wedge.*—Each section displaced progressively forward to the right and left front of the base in the platoon. In assuming this formation in a company of three platoons the base platoon forms inverted wedge; the second platoon forms echelon left; and the third platoon forms echelon right. (See figs. 17 and 33.)

f. Mass.—(1) A formation of the company in line of platoons with intervals and distances of 5 yards.

(2) In higher units masses may be grouped as follows;

(a) *Line of masses.*—Masses abreast with 10-yard interval. (See fig. 34.)

(b) *Column of masses.*—Masses placed one behind another with 10 yards distance between companies. (See fig. 34.)

(c) *Line of battalions, in line of masses.*—Battalions, in line of masses, abreast with 20-yard interval between battalions.

(d) *Line of battalions, in column of masses.*—Battalions in column of masses, abreast with 20-yard interval between battalions.

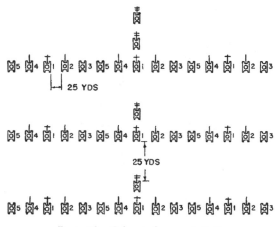

Figure 26.—Column of companies in line.

(e) *Column of battalions, in line of masses.*—Battalions in line of masses, placed one behind another, with distances of 20 yards between battalions.

(f) *Column of battalions, in column of masses.*—Battalions in column of masses, placed one behind another, with distances of 20 yards between battalions.

(3) Mass formations may be used when the company or higher commander desires to give instructions to his unit, and for ceremonies or inspections. When subject to the fire of the enemy, mass formations should never be used.

(4) These formations are gained in the same manner as any other line or column formations on the appropriate commands or signals.

g. To assemble.—(1) Being in disorder or dispersed, the leader commands or signals: ASSEMBLE, and halts or moves slowly forward.

(2) In the section and platoon, all vehicles assemble, in column, in rear of their leader in normal order.

(3) In the company, each platoon is assembled by its platoon leader in an orderly manner. It is then conducted in the most convenient manner toward the company commander, forming line of platoons, unless the signal assemble is followed by the signal for some other formation. The company commander indicates the base platoon and causes it to follow

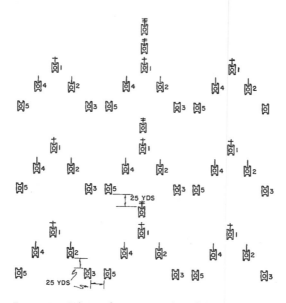

Figure 27.—Column of companies in line of platoons in wedge

him or designates its location; the platoons form in normal order, unless otherwise directed.

h. Movement to flank or rear.—(1) Simultaneous changes in direction of vehicles to either flank or to the rear will be executed on the command or signal: 1. BY THE RIGHT (LEFT) FLANK, 2. MARCH, OR 1. TO THE REAR, 2. MARCH. Vehicles will execute to the rear by turning to the *left* about. Platoon and higher commanders will proceed as rapidly as possible to their positions at the head of their units. Vehicles within the platoon will resume their normal positions upon the next change in formation.

(2) If it is desired to change the direction of larger elements simultaneously, the signals will be those for changing direction preceded by the signal for the element. For example, to have all platoons in a company move to the right flank, the signal will be: 1. PLATOONS, 2. CHANGE DIRECTION TO THE RIGHT, 3. MARCH.

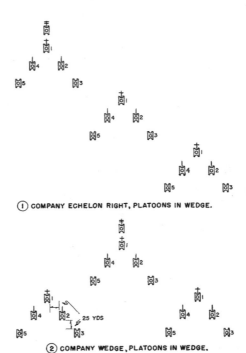

① COMPANY ECHELON RIGHT, PLATOONS IN WEDGE.

② COMPANY WEDGE, PLATOONS IN WEDGE.

Figure 28.

i. Right (left) front into line.—Line may be formed from column on either side of leader by the command: 1. RIGHT (LEFT) FRONT INTO LINE, 2. MARCH, or the signal for LINE followed by pointing to the right (left) front. At this command all leaders and elements move out successively to the right (left) front from column in time to come up abreast on the line formed by the leader when he halts. The interval between vehicles is 5 yards unless otherwise prescribed. (See fig. 35.)

j. To disperse.—(1) To disperse quickly from any formation, at the command or signal DISPERSE, vehicles in a platoon acting alone disperse irregularly so that they are not less than 50 yards from any other vehicle and halt. If the platoon is part of a higher unit, platoons are led by the platoon leaders

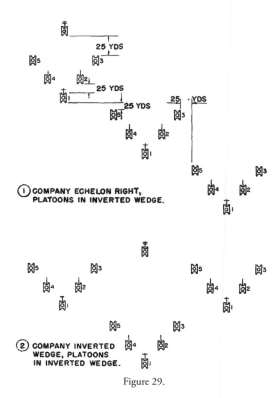

① COMPANY ECHELON RIGHT, PLATOONS IN INVERTED WEDGE.

② COMPANY INVERTED WEDGE, PLATOONS IN INVERTED WEDGE.

Figure 29.

rapidly in different directions and vehicles disperse as in the platoon acting alone. The distance between platoons will not be less than 50 yards.

(2) This movement is for use in any emergency when troops are in a close order or march formation and it is desired to spread out the vehicles rapidly to minimize the effect of a surprise attack by air or artillery fire. Vehicles endeavor to halt under cover and place themselves in positions of readiness to meet any such attack.

k. To follow leader.—(1) To change formation quickly or to bring order out of confusion, the leader moves off in the desired direction and commands or signals: 1. (SUCH) FORMATION, 2. FOLLOW ME.

27

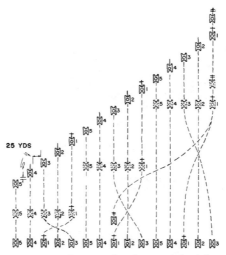

Figure 30.—Company from line to echelon left.

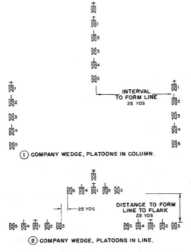

Figure 31.

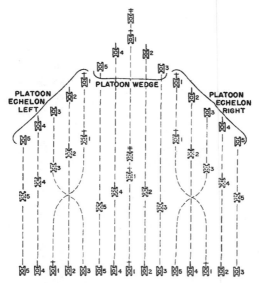

Figure 32.—Company from line to wedge.

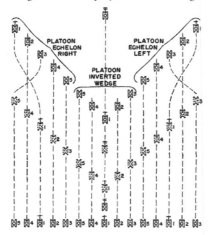

Figure 33.—Company from line to inverted wedge.

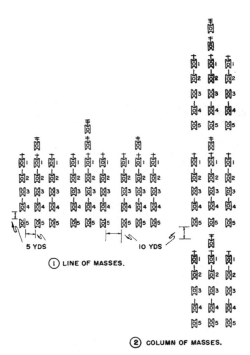

① LINE OF MASSES.

② COLUMN OF MASSES.

Figure 34.

(2) In the platoon, all vehicles move rapidly and take up the designated formation.

(3) In the company, each platoon leader, if the platoon is not in the desired formation, commands or signals: 1. (SUCH) FORMATION, 2. FOLLOW ME, and then conducts it toward the company commander. The platoon first arriving near the company commander becomes the base of the new formation.

l. To rally.—(1) Being in disorder or dispersed, the leader commands or signals: RALLY, and moves slowly forward or halts.

(2) In the platoon, all vehicles move rapidly and form wedges in rear of their leader in any order. Vehicles within the platoon will resume their

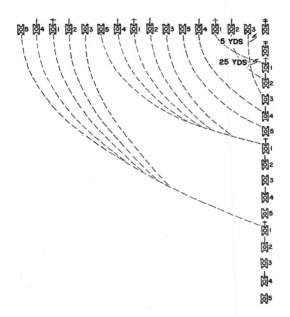

Figure 35.—Company from column to left front into line.

normal positions upon the next change in formation or upon the command assemble.

(3) In the company, each platoon is rallied by its platoon leader while moving and is conducted rapidly toward the company commander, forming line of platoons in wedges. The first platoon to reach the company commander forms in his rear, and other platoons form on the nearest flank.

(4) Rally is used when a rapid reforming is required to renew the attack or to meet an immediate hostile threat.

This excerpt from a German training pamphlet, which was translated and reproduced in the American *Intelligence Bulletin* (December 1942), sets out the methods of intercommunication available to the crew of the Panzer IV.

Operating the Panzer IV

2. Intercommunication

The following means of intercommunication are available:

External: Voice radio and key radio, flag signals, hand signals, signal pistol, and flashlight.

Internal: Intercommunication telephone, speaking tube, and touch signals.

The maximum distance for satisfactory voice radio communication between two moving vehicles is about 3¾ miles, and for satisfactory key radio communication about 6¼ miles.

Flag signals are used for short-distance communications only, and a flashlight is used at night. The signal pistol is used for prearranged signals—chiefly to other arms, such as the infantry.

The radio set, in conjunction with the intercommunication telephone, provides the tank commander, radio operator, and driver with a means for external and internal voice communication. The same microphones and telephone receiver headsets are used in both cases.

When the control switch on the radio is set at *Empfang* (receive), and that on the junction box of the intercommunication telephone at *Bord und Funk* (internal and radio—that is, intercommunication telephone and external voice or key radio), the commander, radio operator, and driver hear all incoming voice radio signals. Any of these men can also speak to the other two after switching his microphone into the circuit by means of the switch on his chest.

For voice radio transmission, the switch on the radio set is adjusted to *Telephonic* (telephone). The telephone switch may be left at *Bord und Funk*. Either the tank commander or the radio operator can then transmit, and both they and the driver will hear the messages transmitted. Internal communication is also possible at the same time, but the conversation will be transmitted.

If the radio set is disconnected or out of order, the telephone switch may be adjusted to *Bord* (internal). The tank commander and driver can then speak to one another, and the radio operator can speak to them, but cannot hear what they say. This also applies when a radio receiver is available, but no transmitter, with the difference that incoming voice radio signals can then be heard by the radio operator.

The signal flags are normally carried in holders on the left of the driver's seat. When the cupola is open, flag signals are given by the tank commander; when it is closed, the loader raises the circular flap in the left of the turret roof and signals with the appropriate flag through the port thus opened. Flag signals are given in accordance with a definite code, the meaning of any signal depending on the color of the flag used and whether the flag is held still or moved in a particular way.

Pistol signals are given through the signal port in the turret roof, through the cupola, or through one of the vision openings in the turret wall. The signal pistol must not be cocked until the barrel is already projecting outside the tank. It is normally used only when the tank is at the halt. The main function of this means of communication is the giving of prearranged signals to the infantry or other troops.

When the tank is traveling at night, with lights dimmed or switched off altogether, driving signals are given with the aid of a dimmed flashlight. The same method is also employed when tanks are in a position of readiness and when leaguered (in bivouac).

Orders are transmitted from the tank commander to the gunner by means of speaking-tube and touch signals. The latter is also used for messages from the commander to the loader, and between the gunner and loader.

The complexities of using the wireless (radio) are demonstrated by this appendix from a 1941 British manual for the Matilda Infantry Tank Marks II, IIA, and IIA*.

Internal Communication Equipment

(a) Description.

The Tank is fitted with a Telephone Set, A.F.V., which enables the Commander to communicate with members of the crew whether wireless is or is not fitted. It is possible that, in the case of later vehicle issues, this telephone equipment may be replaced by Tannoy crew control equipment which employs loud speakers.

A telephone set, A.F.V., comprises:—

A switch unit complete with 4½-volt dry battery.

A hand microphone.

Receivers' headgear (headphones).

Telephone jacks adjacent to each crew member.

Wiring and terminal blocks.

The switch unit Mark II consists of a box with a telephone key switch giving three positions, a microphone transformer, a 4½-volt dry battery, a battery regulating resistance for varying the microphone current, jack sockets and terminals. A switch unit Mark I was fitted to a few early Tanks and differs from the Mark II in that there is no battery regulating resistance for varying the microphone current.

Each "jack telephone" is a metal cylinder 7½ inch longer by 1¼ inch diameter, suspended from a hook adjacent to each crew member. It contains a telephone jack into which can be plugged the Plug, single, No. 9 of a receiver headgear.

There are two leads from each jack. One is connected to a terminal on a hull batten and the other, of copper braid, is earthed.

(b) Switch Positions.

There are three positions for the switch which the Commander, when wireless is fitted, must operate according to whether he wishes to speak to the crew or speak on the main wireless set. The third switch position is not used.

(i) "I.C." position of switch. Rest position.

This allows the Commander to speak to the crew (excluding the wireless operator) and to listen in on the main wireless set. He hears a faint side tone of his own speech.

(ii) A.R/T position of switch.

This allows the Commander to listen or speak on the main wireless set and to speak to the wireless operator.

The crew receive a faint side tone of all communications over the main wireless set, not enough for them to understand the speech but sufficient to know that it is taking place.

(iii) B.R/T.

This position is only used in Tanks equipped with a second wireless set.

(c) Working Instructions.

(i) Plug the appropriate microphone and telephones into the switch unit and jacks and plug the appropriate connectors into the wireless set.

The connectors between wireless and switch unit are part of the wireless set equipment.

(ii) With the key switch of the switch unit at "I.C.", speak into the microphone and ensure that good speech is receivable at all points in the system. Faint side-tone should be received by the Commander in his own headphones when speaking into the microphone.

(iii) Switch the wireless set to "SEND" and adjust the appropriate controls for maximum radiation. Set the key switch of the switch unit to "A.R/T" and ensure that clear speech is being transmitted by adjusting the modulation control on the wireless set and noting the deflection in the aerial current ammeter. Side tone should be received distinctly in the headphones. Adjust the "Mic. Current Increase" knob as required to give the desired speech output.

(iv) Similarly, for reception of wireless signals, adjust the wireless set for reception and ensure that signals are receivable by the Commander through the switch unit.

(d) Maintenance.

Terminals must be kept tight and connections clean. The 4½-volt battery should be tested periodically.

There were simpler ways of getting the message across in a noisy tank, as the handbook for the Light Tank M-2 (in British service) explains. Not all tank crews had radios, and radios were not always reliable, so commanders would develop their own methods for signalling orders to their crew.

Tank Driver's Handbook, Light Tank M-2

SECTION III: Commands and Signals

Touch signals:—

Touch signals are used for communication between the tank commander and the driver. The following code will be used (hand or foot may be used to transmit the signals):—

(a) Move Forward or Increase Speed: Tap repeatedly between shoulder blades.

(b) Move Slower:

1) Rake toe across driver's back horizontally.

or (2) Tap slowly and repeatedly on the driver's head until desired speed is acquired.

(c) Halt:

1) Press firmly on the top of the driver's head.

or 2) Press between shoulder blades below neck.

(d) Change Direction right (or left): Press on the shoulder of the driver on the side which is desired.

(e) Move in Reverse: Pull to the rear on the driver's collar.

Gunnery training was fundamental for all crews; mastery of the firing drills and comprehension of the technical side of gunnery was necessary to enable fast, accurate firing of the gun in combat. As noted by members of the US 1st Armored Regiment on the front line in Tunisia in 1943: 'New men in the armored units should study guns and maps above everything else. You've got to know where you're going and how to get there before you can shoot, and you've got to be able to hit what you shoot at after you get there', and 'Every man must know driving and gunnery. Too many times tanks have had to be abandoned because there was no one left to bring them back after the driver became a casualty, and ammunition has been wasted through ineffectual firing because no one knew how to operate the guns after the gunner became a casualty.' (*Training Notes from Recent Fighting in Tunisia,* March 1943)

Gunnery training for crews would cover the technicalities of the weapons with which their tank was equipped and the types of ammunition available, the selection of targets, and how to estimate and adjust range. The commander would learn to give fire orders to his gunners in a consistent and accurate way, such as laid out in this wartime 3rd Royal Tank Regiment directive.

3. R. Tanks Directive No. 1

Fire Orders

1. Requirements of a fire order are RAPIDITY and BREVITY.
2. Military vocabulary

Tank	...	AFV.
ANT	...	Anti-Tank gun.
MG	...	Machine gun.
MEN	...	Infantry.
MET	...	Transport.
TRENCH	...	Troops under cover.

3. All orders given to the crew by the Comd will be prefaced as follows.

    75 – 37, 6pr, 2pr, How, Co-Ax, Driver, Operator.
4. Commander to driver will be:—

    "DRIVER – RIGHT – ON"

    "DRIVER – SPEED UP – SLOW DOWN – HALT"
5. Whether in tanks or on ground, all targets will be indicated by the "Clock Ray Method".

6. Clock Ray method is as follows:

 e.g. "Reference Point – Eight hundred – right – three o'clock – six degrees – ANT"

7. Degrees can be measured by:—

 Holding the hand out at arms length –

First joint of knuckle.	1 deg.
First two joints.	3 deg.
4 knuckles.	8 deg.
4 fingers spread out.	12 deg.
Span of hand.	16–18 deg.

 Or by graticules in binoculars.

8. When using binoculars it is not advisable to keep the binoculars to the eyes all the time. Only raise the binoculars to the eyes when you hear the shot fired.

9. Range will always be ordered – Six hundred – one thousand – one five hundred – two thousand and so on.

10. Constant practice for Commander and gunner in target recognition and range estimation is VITAL.

11. Essentials of a good fire order are:—

 Definite sequence.

 Omission of unnecessary words.

 Use of military vocabulary.

 Constant practice.

Fire Orders for 75mm Gun

(a) <u>Targets</u>

 H.E. – A/Tk positions, MET and Infantry.

 A.P – A.F.Vs and other armoured vehicles.

(b) <u>Method of ranging</u>

H.E. – Ensure both 75 mm and 37 mm are at ZERO (12 o'clock). Commander looks along barrel of 37 mm and measures switch with binoculars in degrees between the direction in which the 37 mm barrel is pointing and the target. He then orders the 75 mm gunner to traverse his gun on an equivalent number of turns (degrees) in the required direction. The 75 mm gun is now pointing toward the target area. Commander then judges range. The gunner will lay on any point in front of him at the range ordered.

Standard fire order e.g. 75 – H.E. – load, RIGHT 3 turns – Three thousand. One round – Fire.

A.P. – The Commander directs the 75 mm gun on to the target in the same way as for H.E. Difference is that the target is described as it is essential for the gunner to SEE the target.

Standard fire order e.g. 75 – A.P. load. LEFT four turns – One thousand. Turret down tank. One round – fire.

(c) <u>Method of correction.</u>

H.E. – Correction will be by bracket system. Orders will be 'UP ONE TURN', 'DOWN ONE HALF', 'UP ONE QUARTER' and so on giving ONE ROUND FIRE each time. When in the target area go to fire for effect. Order 'THREE ROUNDS GUNFIRE'.

A.P. – Since the gunner can see the target the initial round normally falls very close to the target. Correction will be as follows 'RIGHT ONE TARGET LENGTH', 'DOWN ONE HALF TARGET HEIGHT', 'ONE ROUND FIRE'.

When a direct hit is obtained go to fire for effect.

(d) In an HE shoot it is realised that by getting the gunner on to the target by the 'Clock Ray' Method greater accuracy of the first round is obtained. However this entails a certain amount of time. By getting a round in the ground promptly if slightly inaccurate, it is felt that the speed of engagement of the target outweighs any initial inaccuracy.

(e) <u>Bracket system.</u>

i. Always correct for line first.

ii. Then correct for range. Try and get first shot minus of target, the next shot plus. Then automatic bracketing should take place by halving the previous corrections until the target is hit.

iii. If first shot is out for line and only slightly out for range – correct for line only.

iv. If first shot is far out – be bold in your correction.

v. If target is beyond limits of telescope (3000 yds) say 3800 yds, order will be "THREE THOUSAND – UP TO TWO TURNS". [GOLDEN

RULES FOR RANGING. 1. BE BOLD in your initial correction for range.
2. Correct for LINE FIRST.]

6. <u>Gun Laying</u>.
    (a) Make certain lateral and vertical wire on telescope intersect on target.
Set points to ZERO, then FIRE.
    (b) After first shot relay <u>before</u> applying correction.
    (c) When firing hold elevating wheel to prevent it from moving.
    (d) Observe which number of handwheel is opposite the point so that
in case handwheels move during recoil they can be put back to correct
position before applying next correction.

Fire orders for 6 pr, 2pr, 37 mm, Co-Ax MGs

1. Standard fire order –
    "DRIVER – SLOW DOWN – HALF – 2 PR – TRAVERSE RIGHT –
STEADY – ON – EIGHT HUNDRED – TANK – FIRE"

2. On command 'FIRE' gunnery will carry on firing until further orders. If gunner
is not on the target commander will order 'STOP'. He will then correct gunner.
    'RIGHT ONE HALF TARGET LENGTH', UP ONE TARGET
HEIGHT", 'ONE ROUND FIRE'

3. Commander will carry on correcting and firing ONE ROUND fire until
he is satisfied the gunner is on the target. He will then order "FIRE". Gunner
will then continue firing until further orders.

4. This will not normally apply in the case of Co-Ax MGs since the effective
zone of the gun is so large.

5. If time permits indication of inconspicuous targets will be done by just
putting the gunner on to the target area and then pin pointing the target by
CLOCK RAY METHOD.

6. On some occasions it may be necessary (particularly in GRANTS and
LEES) for commander to concentrate on another weapon (e.g. 75 mm) in
which case the command 'GUN CONTROL' will be given to the 37 mm
gunner who will engage suitable targets at his own discretion.

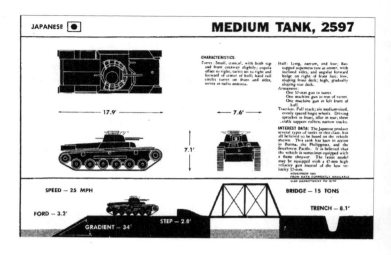

JAPANESE ●

MEDIUM TANK, 2597

CHARACTERISTICS:

Turret: Small, conical, with both top and front cutaway slightly; cupola offset to right; turret set to right and forward of center of hull; hand rail circles turret on front and sides, serves as radio antenna.

← 17.9' →   ← 7.6' →   7.1'

Hull: Long, narrow, and low; flat-topped superstructure at center, with inclined sides, and angular forward bulge on right of front face; low, sloping front deck; high, gradually sloping rear deck.

Armament:
    One 57-mm gun in turret.
    One machine gun in rear of turret.
    One machine gun in left front of hull.

Traction: Full track; six medium-sized, evenly spaced bogie wheels. Driving sprocket in front, idler in rear; three track support rollers; narrow tracks.

INTEREST DATA: The Japanese produce several types of tanks in this class, but all believed to be based on the vehicle shown. This tank has been in action in Burma, the Philippines, and the Southwest Pacific. It is believed that the vehicle is sometimes equipped with a flame thrower. The latest model may be equipped with a 47-mm high velocity gun instead of the low velocity 57-mm.

NOVEMBER 1942
FROM DATA CURRENTLY AVAILABLE
WAR DEPARTMENT FM 30-40

SPEED — 25 MPH   BRIDGE — 15 TONS

FORD — 3.2'   TRENCH — 8.1'

GRADIENT — 34°   STEP — 2.8'

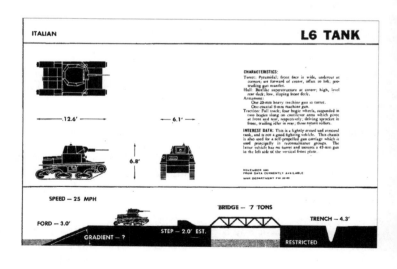

ITALIAN

L6 TANK

CHARACTERISTICS:

Turret: Pyramidal; front face is wide, undercut at corners; set forward of center, offset to left; protruding gun mantlet.

Hull: Boxlike superstructure at center; high, level rear deck; low, sloping front deck.

Armament:
    One 20-mm heavy machine gun in turret.
    One coaxial 8-mm machine gun.

Traction: Full track; four bogie wheels, suspended in two bogies slung on cantilever arms which pivot at front and rear, respectively; driving sprocket in front; trailing idler in rear; three return rollers.

← 12.6' →   ← 6.1' →   6.8'

INTEREST DATA: This is a lightly armed and armored tank, and is not a good fighting vehicle. This chassis is also used for a self-propelled gun carriage which is used principally in reconnaissance groups. The latter vehicle has no turret and mounts a 47-mm gun in the left side of the vertical front plate.

NOVEMBER 1940
FROM DATA CURRENTLY AVAILABLE
WAR DEPARTMENT FM 30-40

SPEED — 25 MPH

FORD — 3.0'   BRIDGE — 7 TONS   TRENCH — 4.3'

GRADIENT — ?   STEP — 2.0' EST.   RESTRICTED

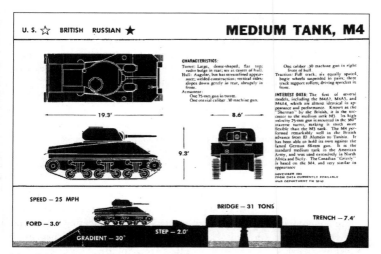

The ability to instantly recognise friendly and enemy armoured fighting vehicles was vital. *FM 30-40: Recognition Pictorial Manual on Armored Vehicles* shows the silhouettes of a wide variety of vehicles, plus visual indications of their capabilities.

The aim in gunnery training was realism. In the US, crews might be trained on 'wobbly plates', oscillating platforms on which tank guns were fixed so they could practice loading, aiming, and shooting the tank gun under 'actual combat conditions', before progressing to aiming at moving targets. In the M4 Sherman, aiming on the move became much easier with the advent of the gyrostabiliser, although it required careful maintenance to work properly. US gunnery practice was to halt to fire, but the stabiliser helped the gunner keep the gun roughly on the target while moving. German and Italian crews similarly were trained to halt to fire their main guns, but early in the war British crews were trained to fire on the move (this was discouraged in 1943), and the Red Army encouraged crews to fire on the move. This article on gunnery is from the official Soviet *Tank Journal* (1939). It criticises the existing training method for teaching gunnery, and propounds a new, more practical programme for teaching gunnery on the move.

Training to Shoot from a Moving Tank

The art of shooting on the move requires particular skill on the part of the gunner, which can only be acquired through intensive training. Whether or not a tankman succeeds in mastering the skill depends on how well this complicated part of his weapons training is taught.

Teaching how to shoot on the move has its own specificities, and it is to these that we would like to draw the reader's attention.

If it is true to say that the success of a soldier's training depends on how much practical experience he receives, then it is all the more so in learning how to shoot on the move.

Take, for example, a topic like learning the characteristics of tank movement.

In normal circumstances the subject would be studied as follows: a trainee would be shown a series of different graphs, neatly drawn on paper, providing a more or less accurate diagrammatic representation of the juddering movement of the vehicle. These would all be accompanied by an array of mathematical calculations, barely comprehensible to a Red Army Soldier.

But worse still is the fact that the majority of time allotted to weapons training is expended on similar exercises. It is believed that after lessons like these the gunner will be able to deal with all the possible tricks that a pitching and rolling tank might throw up.

The fallacy of this approach is plain for all to see.

It is vital that the gunner becomes familiar with the tank's characteristic seesaw motion, but this must be done in practice not on paper.

Normally trainees get used to the oscillatory motion of a tank within the first few days of driving the vehicle. The commanding officer now need only draw the trainees' attention to the most important characteristics of the phenomenon concerning shooting on the move. This can be done in the following way:

Using a bobbing pendulum-like target, explain the constituent features of oscillatory motion: span, attenuation at either end ('dead points') and so on. Next the trainee should try firing a small-calibre weapon (from a practice turret), aiming directly at the centre of the bobbing target. The trainees will see that the bullets will either hit above or below the point at which they took aim. The instructor, using this fact, will explain the concept of firing delay.

All this will be clarified by the methods needed to combat firing delay. The commanding officer should point out to the trainees that a full solution to the issue can only be found through proper training.

Next the methods (procedures) of shooting on the move can be looked at in detail.

The commanding officer explains that in order to fire a tank on the move, it is possible to use the moment at which the line-of-sight matches up to the target when the vehicle is at one of the upper or lower dead points.

Having explained the technique of this method of shooting, the officer running the exercise should let each student fire two to three shots at the target (using a small-calibre weapon), aiming to catch it at the dead points. The gunner should be given free rein to fire without interference from the instructor. Mistakes can be pointed out after each shot. Experience has shown that students will catch on quickly.

Afterwards, the commanding officer remarks that while this method can occasionally produce excellent results, the complexity of a tank's oscillatory movements means that in reality it is difficult to catch the moments of attenuation (dead points).

There are alternative, more commonly used, methods of shooting on the move.

Taking into account the delay, it is possible to fire a shot before the vertical plane has aligned with the target, giving a certain amount of lead time. The length of lead needed depends on the skill of the gunner and the oscillatory motion of the vehicle.

The instructor should again make the trainees practice shooting at a bobbing target (or from an oscillating turret) suggesting that they try to get a feel for the lead time needed for different types of oscillation.

As in the first case, regardless of how well they do, the trainees will understand the essence of this method of shooting on the move within two or three shots.

Now the instructor can add that it is not possible to recommend to the gunner what lead time to give; every gunner should get the hang of this themselves during practice sessions (training).

Next the instructor, moving over to the oscillating turret, explains in detail the procedure of how to aim when shooting on the move.

Some inexperienced gunners, energetically working the sighting mechanism, try to keep the target within their sightline as it jumps around the field of view. This method of aiming from a moving tank leads to bad results because however hard the gunner tries he will never be able to keep up with the oscillations (this can be closely mimicked in a practice turret).

Aiming on the move is best done in the following way: adjust the swivel mechanism so that the horizontal plane is fixed on the target, wait until the oscillatory motion of the tank is on the decrease, that is to say starts to attenuate (show this on the practice turret), and with light turns of the elevating mechanism correct the vertical plane. Then, leaving a certain length of lead time, fire the weapon. This method will give good results.

However, it is often the case that the tank will vibrate intensely all the time and so waiting for a point of attenuation is not an option. If this is the case, quickly adjust the swivel mechanism, and not letting the horizontal plane of the sighting device move away from the target, fire with a lead either above or below the target (whatever is easiest).

All these methods can be demonstrated with the participation of the trainees by shooting from an oscillating turret with small-calibre bullets.

In this way, during a two, three or four hour lesson the most important elements of shooting a tank on the move can be explained and demonstrated.

But tuition should not end here. Intensive, systematic training must follow. Training can be organised in roughly the following way:

a) shooting at a bobbing target with the aid of a marker to help fix the point of attenuation; to make the exercise more varied the characteristics of the swing can be adjusted

b) shooting at a bobbing target with small-calibre bullets

c) elementary shooting drills or their equivalent; with an oscillating turret the levels of difficulty can be varied at the discretion of the instructor

d) Systematic training in how to aim on the move from a military vehicle; for this all the different types of tank movement should be used

It should become a rule that when vehicles are in motion – during tactical exercises, while driving etc. – the tank commander or the turret gunner should sit behind the sighting device and practice laying the gun. It is true that there will not be any supervision of their gun laying, but after the relevant training the gunner will himself get a feel for and try to correct his own mistakes.

Training should be carried out every day; the commanding officer should be assertive and firm in this, not allowing for any disruptions. Otherwise it will be impossible to achieve any degree of success in mastering how to shoot on the move.

The precise order of the elementary lessons can be decided by the commanding officer, but this must be done rationally, so that all, or at least the majority, of the elementary shooting exercises are completed before the start of individual combat shooting practice. If this does not happen, there is a risk that that the trainee will start on the individual combat shooting practice without the necessary training.

Learning the rules of shooting on the move must also take on practical form. This comes about during training and shooting practice. At this time, it should be borne in mind that a difficult aspect of shooting on the move is watching the explosions and discerning their true meaning. For example, it is usual for a gunner to take falling short of his target to mean that he did not correctly range the sighting device, but this might in fact have been the result of mistakes the gunner himself made at the moment of firing. Therefore all instructors should require the trainees to give a report on their expected results. After firing from, for example, a small-calibre weapon (or having marked the angle using a pricking device) a gunner will report 'up', 'down', 'right' and so on. This enables the gunner to develop the necessary skill to evaluate explosions correctly and means that they will have the know-how to correct their line of fire when shooting on the move.

Proficiency in firing on the move depends on the attitude of the tank crew as a whole. In this the mechanic/driver plays an important role.

The mechanic-driver is unlikely to be able to control the vehicle in a manner beneficial to the gunner if he is not familiar with the specifics of shooting on the move. This needs to be taken into account when putting together a tank crew. The driver of a tank, alongside other general duties, must be familiar with the basic rules of shooting on the move.

Unfortunately, in practice this does not always happen and naturally this affects how well a tank will shoot.

The essential point about learning how to shoot on the move is to ensure continuous training with equipment and practical experience in a combat vehicle. All theoretical issues and rules of shooting must be learnt through first-hand experience.

CHAPTER 2: TACTICS

Unlike the rest of his crew, the tank commander needed to understand tactics. He needed to know his tank operated within a unit, and how it would contribute to achieving the objective. As he became more experienced he might rise to command a troop/squadron, at which point a command of tactics would be even more crucial. Tactical training might include theoretical exercises, sand table exercises, carrying out exercises on the ground on foot, and manoeuvres. Manoeuvres gave a commander practice at balancing the many aspects of his role, enabling him to quickly recognise situations, decide on appropriate action and follow through. The tactics that he would be taught to use, and adapt as necessary, would be shaped by the underlying doctrines of the armed forces for which he was fighting.

US LIGHT AND MEDIUM TANK TACTICS

There was limited development of tanks or tactics in the USA in the 1920s, and while the development of new tanks did begin in the early 1930s, it only began to gather pace due to political developments in Europe. The Spanish Civil War, which provoked an arms race in Europe, garnered a slower response in the United States, leaving it behind in tank design. The Fall of France in 1940, and the prominent role of the panzer in the German Blitzkrieg finally led to the creation of the Armored Force, based at Fort Knox. The high proportion of cavalry officers in the new force influenced the Force's tactics and training.

The armoured doctrine that developed was shaped by the success of the Blitzkrieg, with a focus on armoured divisions undertaking mobile warfare, the modern equivalent of a cavalry force. The infantry would break through enemy positions, and the armoured divisions would then exploit the breakthrough and race for the rear. Based on their knowledge of the campaigns in Europe in 1940, tank against tank fighting was not considered likely, instead anti-tank artillery would take on enemy tanks. Upon this basis American tactics and light and medium tanks were developed, tanks that were fast and mobile, but relatively lightly armoured.

FM 17–30

ARMORED FORCE FIELD MANUAL: TANK PLATOON

October 22, 1942

CHAPTER 1: GENERAL

1. PURPOSE AND SCOPE.—a. This manual is written as a guide for the tactical training and combat procedure for the individual tank, the tank section, and the tank platoon, both light and medium. The tactical procedures and methods set forth herein are not to be followed as inflexible rules, as such practice would stifle individual initiative. The methods of procedure given must be varied to meet the particular situation at hand.

b. Key to symbols used in this manual will be found in Figure 1.

2. ORGANIZATION.—The tank platoon, both light and medium, consists of five tanks. The platoon is divided into a platoon headquarters consisting of the platoon leader and the crew of his tank, and two sections of two tanks each.

3. CHARACTERISTICS.—a. The tank is characterized by great mobility, fire power, armor protection, and shock action. These characteristics are possessed in varying degree by different types of tanks. The characteristics dictate the manner of employment. All types of tanks are limited by their restricting vision devices.

b. Light tanks, as compared to medium tanks, have less fire power, lighter armor and armament, greater speed, and better maneuverability. They are particularly fitted for—

(1) feeling out and developing weak spots in the enemy position through which medium tanks may attack.

(2) Screening the advance against light enemy resistance.

(3) Leading an attack against an unarmored enemy weak in antitank defense, when speed is essential.

(4) A fast maneuvering force to exploit the success of other tanks.

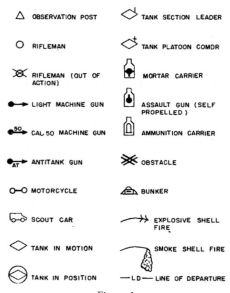

Figure 1

(5) Maneuver to flank or rear to strike the enemy command posts, communications centers, reserves, and vital installations.

(6) Pursuing a defeated enemy.

c. Medium tanks, because of their greater fire power, guns of heavier calibre, increased armor protection, and shocking power are used to—

(1) Lead an attack against an enemy whose position and strength are known.

(2) Support by fire the attack of either light or medium tanks.

d. It is essential that tank crew members know the strength and weakness of their tank and its weapons. Furthermore, they must know the strength of their weapons as compared to enemy weapons likely to be encountered.

4. OPERATION.—The tank platoon is the smallest tank battle unit. It normally operates as part of the tank company. However, it may operate as an independent unit as advance, flank, or rear guard or on similar missions.

a. Methods.—Tanks operate by surprise, fire and maneuver, and in mass. The violation of these fundamentals will lead to ineffectual effort and perhaps disaster.

(1) *Surprise.*—Surprise is gained by striking the enemy at an unexpected time, from an unexpected direction, with all strength possible. Speed of movement, use of covered approaches, and coordination of fires assist in gaining surprise. *Seek to surprise the enemy but do not let yourself be surprised. Give the enemy credit for being as capable as yourself. Do not underestimate his ability. Do not become careless. Expect the unexpected and be prepared for it.*

(2) *Fire and maneuver.*—An advancing unit is covered by the fire of weapons in stationary position. This is important as the tank in the open is not only extremely vulnerable but movement, dust, and restricted vision make the locating of new targets extremely difficult. Tanks in defiladed position can quickly locate and promptly bring fire upon hostile weapons that fire upon the advancing tanks. This procedure of fire and movement may be by section, platoon, or company.

(3) *Mass.*—Concentrate effort. Do not waste strength on numerous unimportant targets. Strike on a key position with all power that can be mustered. If this falls, others may then be taken. If effort is made on several positions, the enemy may easily destroy you by concentrating successively on each attacking element.

b. Coordination.—Coordination of effort, that is, timing of all elements, is essential. An uncoordinated effort violates the fundamental of the use of mass. Therefore, in attack, time the movement of the tanks and the opening of fire by supporting weapons or supporting tanks so that maximum effect is obtained. Teamwork is essential.

c. Initiative and aggressiveness.—In order to obtain success in battle, leaders must exercise initiative and act aggressively. A small force acting under direction of an aggressive, alert leader can overcome a much larger force whose leader is slow and nonaggressive. Do not let the enemy have time to get set. Conversely, do not rush headlong into battle with no plan of action. Think clearly, give clear orders, *then* act fast.

d. Striking weakness.—Seek to strike the enemy where he is weak in antitank defense. Do not drive headlong against strong antitank defense. Bypass it or call for assistance to reduce it.

e. Mission and echelons of attack.—(1) The mission of tanks in the armored division is to attack and destroy vital hostile installations such as command posts, communication centers, supply installations, reserves, and artillery.

(2) The mission of tanks in the separate tank battalions is to assist infantry, cavalry, or motorized divisions to advance by destroying hostile machine guns, personnel, and vital installations.

(3) A tank attack will usually be launched in three echelons, each echelon in a series of waves.

(a) The first echelon of attack, preceded by neutralization by combat aviation and artillery, if available, is directed against the antitank defenses, artillery, command posts, and other rear installations. (See FM 17–33 and FM 17–32.) Tank platoons of this echelon destroy first the enemy antitank defenses and second, enemy artillery. They attack enemy infantry only when hindered by it in fulfilling their primary missions.

(b) The platoons of the second echelon follow the first echelon at such distance that the enemy will not have time to re-form his antitank defenses. These platoons destroy hostile automatic guns and personnel and clear the way for the advance of infantry. Antitank guns passed over by the first echelon must be silenced by the leading waves of the second echelon.

(c) The tank platoons of the third echelon advance with the infantry, destroy hostile machine guns passed over by the second echelon, and hostile personnel. The mission of this echelon is to assist the advance of the infantry. They may lead the infantry attack if resistance is still heavy. If resistance has been broken by the first two echelons, tanks of the third echelon will follow the infantry, prepared to attack isolated resistance as necessary. These tanks also protect the infantry from counterattack, particularly of mechanized forces.

CHAPTER 2: CREW TRAINING

SECTION I: GENERAL

5. GENERAL.—*a.* The subject of training is covered generally in FM 21–5. In the tank platoon the individual man plays an important role. During the progress of an infantry or cavalry attack the commander is able, by personal contact, to command his troops. In the tank the commander cannot see his men face to face. The platoon leader must rely upon radio and signals for controlling his platoon. The tank attack progresses rapidly and the commander is not able personally to influence the action as well as can commanders of other units. Once the tank attack has started, success depends largely upon the training and

initiative of the individual tank commander. For this reason the training of tank crews must be thorough. Each individual must know his job thoroughly and teamwork of the tank crew must be developed to a high degree.

b. (1) The training of the tank crew, section, and platoon includes—

    (a) Use of terrain.

    (b) Selection of weapons and ammunition.

    (c) Communication and control.

    (d) Reconnaissance.

    (e) Marches and bivouacs.

    (f) Security

    (g) Offensive action.

    (h) Defensive action.

(2) Prior to training in these subjects, individual training and marksmanship (see FM 17–12) should have been completed. Combat practice firing follows tactical training of the crew. (See FM 17–15.) Tank crew drill is covered in FM 17–5.

6. TRAINING PROCEDURE.— The only purpose of tactical training is to prepare for battle. Practical exercises, therefore, are a vital part of training and are, in fact, a dress rehearsal for combat. Solutions of tactical situations should not be stereotyped, otherwise individual initiative is lost. There is usually more than one suitable solution to a tactical problem. Emphasis should be placed upon initiative and aggressive action. Once a decision is made, act quickly, boldly, and vigorously. The following procedure will be used in the preparation and execution of tactical training exercises:

a. The officer in charge of training by map study selects the area, personally reconnoiters the ground, and drafts the problem. With other officers he plays the problem on a map.

b. The problem is next played on a sand table, using numbered blocks of wood or miniature tanks to represent vehicles. (See TF 7–265 and 7–266.) If the problem is for individual tanks, the whole tank crew is present. If for the section or platoon, the noncommissioned officers and selected privates are present. The problem should be run several times and each man called upon for solutions. Interest is maintained by injecting small situations as the action progresses. Emphasize decisions and immediate vigorous action.

c. Following the sand table phase, the section or platoon executes the problem on the ground. After completing the problem, assemble all personnel and hold a critique. Point out errors and state a method of correcting these errors. Avoid ridicule. Repeat the problem as necessary.

SECTION II: TERRAIN

7. STUDY.—The estimate of terrain generally is covered in FM 101–5.

a. The importance of the study of terrain cannot be over-emphasized. Battles are won or lost by the ability of the leader to estimate terrain and use it to his own advantage. The study of terrain must be continuous throughout all phases of training. Each individual must understand thoroughly how to use terrain to his own advantage and must appreciate how the enemy can use it.

b. The study of terrain must be preceded by a thorough course in map and aerial photograph reading. Each individual must be taught the name of terrain features and then the method of converting these features to his advantage. Each individual must answer the following questions:

(1) What is the nature of the soil?

(2) Is it hard or soft? Will the tank sink in a short distance and then be able to move forward, or is there a crust which may carry the vehicle for a short distance and then break, bogging the machine?

(3) Is the ground level or rolling?

(4) Is the surface eroded, forming natural barriers around which a route must be reconnoitered?

(5) Are stream banks soft and swampy, or hard? Steep or sloping?

(6) Are stream bottoms hard sand or gravel, or soft mud?

(7) What is the depth of the stream? Consider not only the depth to the actual bottom but also the amount the tank may sink. Know the fording depth of the tank.

(8) What is the type of vegetation? Does it provide concealment from air observation? From ground observation?

(9) Does terrain afford good firing positions for support of maneuvering tanks? Does it afford concealed routes of approach?

(10) Is the terrain heavily forested or covered only with light brush?

(11) What is the background for an attack? Will the tank be silhouetted against the sky or a light-colored field?

(12) Are there any defiles that will limit your movement?

c. Following is one procedure for study of terrain:

(1) By use of a sand table, teach terrain features and how to use them. (See par. 8.) For use of sand table, see TF 7–265 and TF 7–266.

(2) On the ground, walk the platoon over the terrain. Point out terrain features, show how to use covered approaches and firing positions. Demonstrate testing of swampy ground and fording depth of streams.

(3) Have the platoon drive through the area in tanks; first with ports open and then with ports closed.

8. USE.—*a.* Foot troops use cover to minimize losses in approaching the enemy. The tank, although armored, must also make use of cover when practicable. The following factors render this operation difficult:

(1) The tank forms a much larger target than the foot soldiers and cannot take advantage of small cover. Therefore, it is necessary that routes be carefully chosen.

(2) The speed of the tank reduces the time available for selection of routes while moving. This difficulty is overcome to some extent by choosing, while in turret defilade, a route to a new position.

(3) View from the tank is limited and good routes may be difficult to choose. This may be overcome to some extent by the tank commander observing from the open turret except when under fire.

(4) The formation of the platoon or company may at times preclude maximum use of cover as tanks should not, without the platoon leader's authority, stray more than 50 yards from their assigned direction except when necessary to silence an antitank gun.

(5) The driver, in seeking cover, must coordinate his action with the gunner. Sudden changes or frequent unannounced changes of direction will seriously impair the aim of the gunner.

b. Incorrect and correct methods of using terrain.

Passing a treeless hill. Do not cross the crest of a treeless hill when it can be avoided. Drive around the hill.

Passing a treeless ridge. Do not cross a treeless ridge when it can be avoided. Make use of the ridge as cover for a change of approach direction.

Method of crossing the ridge when detour is impracticable. Do not approach the crest of an extended ridge in deep formation. The enemy can destroy your tanks one by one. Approach the crest in line formation; then all tanks of the platoon reach the crest at the same time and are prepared to concentrate their fire against the enemy battery or antitank gun which may be in position behind the ridge.

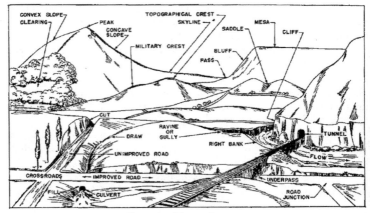

Figure 2.—Terrain features.

Take advantage of folds in the ground. Do not drive straight across country without taking advantage of folds in the ground. Make use of small depressions and valleys.

Driving through closed terrain. Do not drive in broad formation through closely covered terrain; contact is thus very easily lost. Form platoon in double or single column.

Take advantage of lightly wooded areas. During the approach, do not drive by a lightly wooded area. Use the woods for concealment.

Take advantage of buildings. Do not attack without using the house for cover.

Use dark background. Do not drive over a light-colored field when it can be avoided. Use dark background as far as possible for movement.

Stay on dark ground. Do not take a shortcut over a light-colored field. *A* track is left which is visible to enemy observers for hours. Go around the field, thus preventing telltale tracks.

Use dark background. Do not advance in front of a white background. Use dark background to cover advance.

Passing through woods. Do not pass through a dense forest in double column or wider formation. This necessitates the clearance of several paths and contact may be lost. Pass through dense woods in one column and clear only one path.

Avoid open fields. Do not take a short cut across open fields. Go around open fields in order to advance under cover.

Avoid positions on open hills. Do not take position on top of a hill. Take position on the slope, giving defilade to the tank hull.

Concealed position in brush. Do not take position *near* bushes. Drive into the bushes and take position.

Passing through fog. Do not drive through fog in a broad formation, as contact may be lost. Drive through fog in double column in order to narrow and shorten the formation.

Driving through smoke cloud. Do not drive through smoke cloud in wedge formation. As the tanks come out of the smoke cloud the enemy can destroy them one after the other. Drive through a cloud in line formation. The tank platoon comes out of the cloud all together, ready to fire. If defiladed or concealed positions can be taken up until smoke cloud passes, do so. (See FM 17–32.)

Passing through a defile. Spread out as soon as defile is passed in order to bring more fire power to bear on the enemy and to offer a less concentrated target.

Crossing obstacles such as ditches. If an obstacle is crossed in column, much time is lost, for all vehicles must wait until the tank ahead is across. When an obstacle is crossed on a wide front, each vehicle requires the same time. The column then can be quickly re-formed.

SECTION III: WEAPONS AND AMMUNITION

9. GENERAL.—The tank is armed with several weapons of different calibers each of which is provided with more than one type of ammunition. The tank crew must be carefully trained in the characteristics of these weapons, their capabilities and limitations, and the proper use of each. The gunner and tank commanders must know instinctively what weapons to use and the proper type of ammunition for each target.

10. DESCRIPTION.—*a.* depending upon the type of tank, the weapons available are the calibre .30 machine gun, the 37-mm gun, and the 75-mm gun. In addition, the tank has 23 grenades, fragmentation, incendiary, and smoke, and the individual weapons of the crew, submachine gun and pistol.

b. The machine gun is an antipersonnel weapon. When fired from a stationary tank it may be effective at ranges up to 2,500 yards. However, it will normally not be used beyond 1,000 yards. From a moving tank not equipped with the gyro stabilizer, the machine gun should not be used at ranges greater than 300 yards. With the gyro stabilizer, ranges are the same as from a stationary tank. The M1919A4 caliber .30 machine gun cannot deliver sustained fire like the M1917 water-cooled gun. Caliber .30 armor piercing ammunition will penetrate the shield of antitank weapons at 200 yards.

c. The 37-mm gun has three types of ammunition: cannister, high explosive, and armor piercing.

(1) Cannister ammunition is used against personnel at ranges up to 200 yards. (See FM 23–80 and FM 23–81.)

(2) High explosive ammunition is used against unarmored weapons in position, such as machine guns or antitank guns, from an unprotected side. It is no good against armored vehicles or bunkers.

(3) 37-mm armor piercing ammunition is effective against most hostile light and medium tanks up to a range of 800 yards. It is also used against emplacements.

d. The 75–mm gun is equipped with armor piercing, high explosive, and smoke shell.

(1) Armor piercing ammunition is effective against most hostile tanks up to a range of 1,600 yards. The armor piercing shell itself is effective against unarmored vehicles beyond limit of vision of the firer, normally 2,500 to 3,000 yards.

(2) High explosive ammunition is used against antitank guns, machine-gun emplacements, and occasionally against personnel. It is effective beyond the limit of vision (see (1) above). By indirect fire with an observer, it may be used at ranges of 7,500 yards.

(3) Smoke ammunition is effective as in (1) and (2) above. It is used to screen antitank guns so that the tank may move to a more favorable position. The smoke cloud from this projectile is effective 50 yards downwind and the smoke element burns for 10 seconds. The smoke is placed in front of or on the target. For the greatest effect, fire to the windward and just in front of the target.

If wind direction cannot be determined, fire just in front of the target on the line tank-target. Note direction of smoke cloud and fire another shell if necessary. If wind is blowing indirectly toward you, fire in or just behind the target. The smoke shell is also effective against personnel and is incendiary.

11. CONSERVATION OF AMMUNITION.—Each exercise schedule for company training must include training in ammunition conservation. Although exercises are conducted without ammunition, this subject must always be kept in mind. During exercises, the 37-mm and 75-mm gunner should be required to simulate firing and assistant gunners should keep track of the number of rounds the gunner simulated firing. When all ammunition is fired, the gunner ceases firing. This is one of the principal ways in which troops can be trained in conservation of ammunition. If promiscuous simulated firing without thought of ammunition supply is permitted, wasteful habits will be developed. The tank commander requires frequent reports from gunners concerning ammunition supply. The chart below shows in a startling manner what a comparatively small amount of ammunition is available.

Weapons	Rounds carried	Usable rate of fire per minute per weapon	Number of minutes ammunition will last, firing at usable rate	Number of targets that can be engaged with ammunition available at 5 rounds per target
Light tank M3: 3 caliber .30 machine guns	4,000	125	10	
1 37-mm gun	103	10	10	21
Medium tank M3: 2 caliber .30 machine guns	4,000	125	16	
1 37-mm gun	150	10	15	30
1 75-mm gun	50	6	8	10
Medium tank M4: 2 caliber .30 machine guns	4,000	125	16	
1 caliber .50 machine guns	300	125	2.5	
1 75-mm gun	96	6	16	15

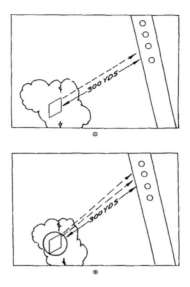

Figure 24.—Firing on foot troops from a moving tank.

Firing on a point target from moving target. Without a gyro stabilizer, do not fire from a moving tank at a point target 300 yards distant (see par. 10b). This is a waste of ammunition. Fire from stationary tank. Move nearer if it is only an enemy machine gun.

Firing on foot troops from a moving tank. Do not fight advancing enemy infantry from a *moving* tank at a range of 500 yards or greater, if suitable stationary firing positions are available. Shoot from stationary tank with machine guns; move the tank forward after the enemy has started to take cover.

Attacking a column of foot troops or horse cavalry. Do not attack a dismounted column with the slow-firing 37-mm gun with armor piercing or high explosive shell: the effect will not be great enough. Make a surprise attack with the fast-firing machine gun. If the column is within 200 yards, use 37-mm canister.

Attacking hostile antitank gun which is firing at some other target. When you are not under fire, do not fire at 500 yards, or greater range, from a moving tank at an enemy antitank gun which is firing at some other target. The effect of your fire is too uncertain and discloses your position. Go into position at once and shoot with all guns at the crew of the antitank gun; the effect of fire from a stationary tank at 800 yards is excellent.

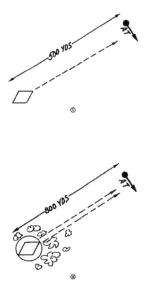

Figure 27.—Attacking hostile antitank gun that is firing at another target.

Attack more dangerous target. Do not shoot at a larger but less dangerous target (ammunition section) while an enemy antitank gun is moving into position. Attack at once; fire with all guns at the enemy antitank gun.

Firing at an antitank gun going into position. Do not fire with a machine gun at an antitank gun going into position at ranges in excess of 800 yards. Fire with the 37-mm or 75-mm gun at the antitank gun going into position.

Attacking an antitank gun frontally. Do *not* attack an antitank gun frontally at 350 yards or greater distance by machine-gun fire. The machine-gun projectiles do not penetrate the armor plates at ranges greater than 350 yards.

Firing at a hostile antitank gun. Do *not* fire with only the 37-mm gun at any enemy antitank gun (400 yards away) pointing in another direction. Fire with all guns at the unprotected flank of the antitank gun.

Firing at hostile antitank gun. Do *not* fire at antitank gun with 37-mm tank gun at close range. It is sufficient to use the machine gun, as armor piercing machine-gun ammunition will penetrate the armor plate at short ranges.

Attacking enemy tanks. When an oncoming enemy tank is met, do not keep moving toward it, firing during movement, if suitable stationary positions are available. Move into position at once and take the enemy tank under fire with armor piercing projectiles from your stationary tank.

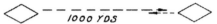

① Do *not* attack an enemy tank with the 37-mm tank gun at more than 800 yards. This is a waste of ammunition.

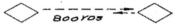

② Let enemy tank approach to within at least 800 yards range.

FIGURE 34.—Firing at hostile tanks.

Figure 34.—Firing at hostile tanks.

① Do *not* attack an enemy tank with explosive shells.

② Fire with armor piercing shells.

Figure 35.—Attacking enemy tanks.

Attacking hostile machine guns. Do *not* fire at an enemy machine gun, not emplaced, with the slow-firing 37-mm tank gun using high explosive or armor piercing shell. This is a waste of ammunition. Eliminate the enemy machine-gun crew by fast-firing machine guns or use 37-mm cannister if within 200 yards.

Attacking an emplaced machine gun. Do not fight an emplaced machine gun with a machine gun. Use 37-mm or 75-mm explosive or armor piercing ammunition.

Attacking a hostile machine gun at close range. Do not try to destroy the crew of an enemy machine gun at close range with explosive shells. At close range, use machine guns to destroy living targets. If range is less than 200 yards, use cannisters.

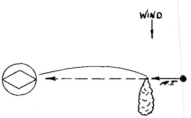

① When the wind is blowing from the side, do *not* aim smoke shell at the front of the target.

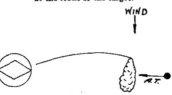

② Aim the shell to the windward side. The wind will blow the smoke in front of the target.

Figure 41.—Use of smoke shell, flank wind.

① When the wind is blowing from your front, do *not* place the smoke shell in front of the target. This does not blind the antitank gun.

② In this case, place the shell behind the target; then the wind will screen it completely.

Figure 42.—Use of smoke shell, head wind.

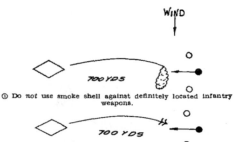

① Do *not* use smoke shell against definitely located infantry weapons.

② Destroy infantry weapons by high explosive shells and ricochet firing.

Figure 43.—Use of smoke shell against small arms.

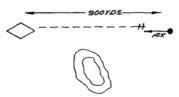

① While changing position, do not answer antitank gun fire with explosive shells.

① Blind the antitank gun immediately with smoke shell, proceed to the next position, and from there destroy the antitank gun with explosive shell.

Figure 44.—Use of smoke shell to cover maneuver.

Firing at loopholes in a bunker. Do not fire with a machine gun at loopholes of the bunker. This will probably not be successful. Destroy the loopholes by 37-mm or 75-mm tank gun fire, using armor piercing projectiles.

BRITISH ARMY TANK BATTALION TACTICS

After the horrors of the First World War, it was almost inevitable that avoiding trench warfare in a future war would be a significant concern in Britain.

The solution pioneered by J. F. C. Fuller and B. H. Liddell Hart was the creation of a mobile army, built around the tank. Although their theories were widely studied abroad, they met some resistance at home. Progress was slowed by the government's Ten Year Rule, in effect until 1932, which assumed the Empire would not fight a major war for ten years and reduced defence spending accordingly. After extensive study and experimentation, the General Staff ended up with two categories of tank in the mid 1930s. These were the infantry tank, slow and heavily armoured, which operated in infantry tank units to support dismounted infantry; and the cruiser tank, which was fast and lightly armoured, organised in armoured units and intended to pursue the enemy and exploit breakthroughs. Light tanks were used for reconnaissance and escort duties. These very different roles required not only different tanks, but also different tactics. The result was that an armoured unit was unlikely to be able to readily support infantry, nor would an army tank unit undertake the role of an armoured unit. Debate over the best way to employ tanks, what type of tank to deploy, and cooperation between armour and other arms continued at the highest levels of the army almost throughout the war.

This is the third part of the training pamphlet for army tank battalions (1939). Parts I and II covered crew and battle drill respectively. This part gives the broader picture of how a tank or troop would fit into the larger strategy, integrating with infantry and artillery.

Military Training Pamphlet No. 22, Part III

Tactical Handling of Army Tank Battalions—Employment

Section 1.—The Army Tank Battalion

1. *Function*

Army Tank Battalions are army troops organized, equipped and trained for employment with formations of all arms.

Army tank units are equipped with tanks possessing heavy armour, relatively low speed and high obstacle-crossing power. They have no weapons for their own close support other than their smoke projectors, nor have they special reconnaissance sections. Thus they are not designed to act independently but in co-operation with infantry and artillery.

By virtue of its high degree of fire power, mobility and protection, the infantry tank is pre-eminently an offensive weapon of great effect in battle.

2. *Equipment*

(i) *Armoured fighting vehicles.*—Infantry tanks of continually improving design are in course of production and issue. Tactical training at present must be based on the characteristics of the Infantry tank, Marks I and II. The important characteristics are the effective armour-protection of the fighting cab, crushing power and the limiting effect of soft or hilly ground.

(ii) *Other vehicles.*—The war establishment of staff cars, carriers, motor cycles and trucks and procedures for their use is given in Part II.

(iii) *Armament.*—The armament of the Infantry Tank, Mark II, is a 2-pr gun and a co-axial M.G.

Tanks armed only with medium machine guns have considerable limitations compared with tanks armed with an A.P. weapon and tactical training must be influenced by this. A true estimate of the effect of fire from tanks under battle conditions, and of the effect of the use of smoke projectors, is necessary to sound tactical handling.

3. *Intercommunication.*—Infantry tanks have the following methods of inter-communication:—

(i) R/T and W/T. The normal method of control from battalion headquarters down to individual tanks in action. A high degree of skill and signal discipline is necessary to obtain the best result.

(ii) Flag, lamp and semaphore, with the company when not under battle conditions.

(iii) Flags from tank to infantry and a call up sign when circumstances permit its use.

4. *Organization.*—An Army Tank Battalion is organized as follows:—

Battalion Headquarters	Infantry tanks	2
	Light tanks	4
3 *Companies*, each of		
H.Qs. 5 *Sections* of 3	Infantry tanks	16
Infantry tanks each.	Light tanks	1
Total for each Coy.		

5. Personnel.—The first essential for tank personnel is high morale, an individual pride in his own and his crew's efficiency and a determination never to let the team down. This is based on sound individual training. Here the first

requirement is each officer's and man's complete mastery of his particular role, gunner, driver, R/T operator or D.R. The second is that every officer and man understands so thoroughly the battle task of his crew, his section, his company and of the other arms that in the face of the enemy he can act as required with a minimum of orders. The third requirement is that every officer and man must learn enough of driving and maintenance, gunner and R/T to be able to replace a casualty in a crew at need.

A high standard of leadership on the part of sub-unit and tank commanders is essential, since occasions will frequently arise when they will be called on to exercise great initiative and make important decisions when reference to higher authority is impracticable.

Crew commanders must be skilful in appreciating and using ground and employing their fire power and armour to achieve their object with economy: they must know the powers and limitations of enemy anti-tank weapons and A.F.Vs. Commanders of army tank units must keep abreast of developments of tactics and equipment both in their arm, other branches of the Service and in foreign armies.

Section 2. Principles of Employment

1. *Co-operation:*—The full power of an army can be exerted only when all its parts combine in action. An army tank unit is only one member of the team working under the orders of the commander of the formation to which they may be allotted.

Infantry tanks are a supporting weapon, and though they will usually provide the leading wave in an attack, their object is to assist the infantry to gain and hold the objective.

Commanders of tank units must understand thoroughly the work of the infantry, artillery and co-operating air force. The efficiency of their co-operation depends on the following personal qualities: adaptability, good humour, quick understanding and the ability quickly to state, justify and adjust their requirements.

2. *Suitable conditions for co-operation.*—Tank battalion and company commanders will be required to advise and assist formation commanders in considering plans for co-operation. This demands beforehand careful study of the map and air photographs and much anticipatory reconnaissance forward.

When consulted, the following principles of employment will guide them in advising on the plan most suitable for the full co-operation of the tanks:—

Concentration of tanks at the decisive point.

Surprise.

Suitable ground.

Adequate support from other arms.

The principle of concentration of strength at the decisive point applies to the employment of tanks with the same force as it does to the employment of any other arm.

Surprise is obtained by bringing tanks forward under cover of darkness or fog, and at the last possible moment, and by the choice of a suitable zero.

Full value cannot be obtained from tanks unless they are employed on suitable ground which should provide hard firm going and freedom from natural tank obstacles. It will be of additional advantage if the ground is such as to provide natural defilade to the flanks of the attack, and to allow of the selection of visible objectives.

Adequate support from artillery, infantry and aircraft during the advance is essential to enable tanks to overcome modern anti-tank defence.

The plan for an attack in which infantry tanks are employed must take into full account the requirements set out above. In return for consideration of these principles, tank commanders must be ready to adjust their plans in detail to the needs of the other arms.

3. *Co-operation in action.*—A junior commander will often be faced with situations requiring a quick decision even sometimes involving deviation from his original orders. To enable him to arrive at a correct solution with rapidity, he must understand clearly the object of the operation and the needs of the infantry with whom he is working.

Section 3: Protection

1. *General.*—A primary duty of every commander is the security of his own unit. A tank unit is at all times liable to ground or air attack in varying degree.

The location of tanks is valuable information to the enemy. Their concealment is of special importance.

2. *Protection in harbour and at halts.*

(i) The tank unit commander has to strike the balance between the requirements of his command in maintenance and rest and the degree of protection necessary to be effective. He will bear in mind the degree of likelihood of attack and the disposition of neighbouring troops, co-ordinating his own local defence with theirs.

(ii) *Protection against air attack.*—The best means of protection is conceal-ment under cover of vehicles and personnel. Close harbour in small patches of cover is liable if discovered to bring down concentrations of bombing and artillery fire if within range, and as much dispersal as is consistent with ground security and control will be adopted at all times. Air sentries will be posted to give the alarm and at all times to ensure that proper concealment is maintained.

Anti-aircraft light machine guns will be mounted and gunners detailed ready to engage low-flying enemy aircraft. Gas sentries will also be posted.

(iii) *Protection against ground attack.*—In harbour and at halts guard tanks, as required, will be posted to command approaches and to remain closed except for top flap and vizors, with crew at action stations, guns loaded and an observer always on duty.

Anti-tank rifles of unit transport should at all times be suitably disposed to engage enemy A.F.Vs. attacking by surprise. Men will be detailed to man these guns at once on the alarm being given.

Anti-aircraft light machine guns can also be used for repulsing ground attacks.

3. *Protection on the move.*

(i) *Protection against aircraft.*—It will be normal for tank units to march by night and all must be able to move without lights. When lights are permissible, their use will conform to the practice of other military vehicles.

By night it is preferable to move across country or in by-roads. Where it is necessary to move by day on roads, tanks will seek concealment by marching at low density in small bodies of irregular size, or with single tanks interspersed with normal traffic.

Halts will be in natural cover where available, dispersed, air sentries be-ing mounted transport A.A. light machine guns being mounted ready for action.

(ii) *Protection against ground attack.*—If tanks on the march are liable to attack or ambuscade, they will move in such formation that tanks are contin-uously inter-supporting and will, if considered necessary, march closed down. In any case, when in proximity of the enemy, one tank will be detailed as guard tank to be closed down except for the top flap and vizors and at all times ready for instant action. The guard tanks should be changed at each halt and remain in a suitable position of observation covering approaches. The rearmost tanks must at all times be ready to fire to the rear.

4. *Concealment.*—Concealment of tracks made by tanks near halts is most important. They are very obvious in air photos. Swinging near cover especially on soft ground must be avoided. Road approach should be used where possible and, across country, tanks should follow in leader's track. A.D.R. should be employed for spotting and covering up any such track marks.

Movement of tanks into and out of harbours during times of good air visibility should be avoided.

Natural cover, small copses, hedges, scrub, and the use of deep shadows, are the best protection against air attack if carefully used. Where no such cover exists, the following devices help:—

(i) Camouflage nets, with possible use of herbage as on the site, particularly to cover up driving track plates.

(ii) Irregular dispersion with tanks pointing at various angles.

(iii) Parking of tanks close together in small groups and sheeted to resemble dumps.

Section 4. Information

1. *General.*—Full and detailed information is required for planning an attack by an army tank battalion. Time available after a decision has been made to attack in a particular sector may be short. Therefore the collection and dissemination of information beforehand concerning likely areas of operation is important. Brigade, battalion and company reconnaissance officers must be specially trained for this duty.

2. *Information concerning the enemy.*—Information of enemy anti-tank methods and weapons and of the general disposition of the enemy must be sought from forward troops and air liaison officers and from the study of air photographs. Such information affecting infantry tanks (e.g., artillery dispositions, anti-tank mine fields, defended localities, wire obstacles, tank obstacles) will be recorded on maps down to crew commanders before the battalion is engaged. This helps to shorten orders.

3. *Anticipatory ground reconnaissance.*—Warning of the possibility of Infantry tank action in any particular sector may of necessity at times be given late. All likely sectors, as indicated by liaison and intelligence officers will be reconnoitred

and plans made for company and section commanders carefully to study these sectors, first, from large scale maps and air photos (particularly obliques) and later, whenever possible, in person. During each phase of an action all commanders will seize every opportunity of reconnoitring areas where further action is possible.

4. *Reconnaissance of assembly areas and harbours.*—Assembly areas and harbours must be reconnoitred well in advance of the time at which they are required to be used and the information passed to the tank units concerned early enough to ensure that tanks will not be checked before moving into cover and thus be discovered from the air. Company guides will precede units to collect the information and direct units to their positions. Reconnaissance of harbours should always include reconnaissance of alternative positions and routes to them.

5. *Reconnaissance of approaches.*—It will often be necessary for tanks to march across country to assembly areas or starting lines. Battalion and company reconnaissance officers will be required to reconnoitre such routes, often in limited time, and to arrange for guiding the tanks there, frequently by night. All officers and D.Rs. must be trained in carrying out such reconnaissances, in marking routes and acting as guides.

A careful study of the map will be of assistance especially if the type of country is well known. Methodical reconnaissance by car or motor cycle is however necessary before a night move can be undertaken.

Reconnaissance officers must be familiar with the performance of their tank units by night and by day. They will be responsible for timing moves and must remember to allow the necessary margin for checks to ensure that the operation is not frustrated by late arrival of the tanks.

For such reconnaissances it is useful if the officers and D.Rs. have some means of accurately measuring the width of bridges or narrow passages.

Part II deals with the procedure to ensure timely and smooth routine on approach marches.

Section 5. Attack

1. *General.*—Army tanks are essentially an arm of attack to be used to precede and accompany infantry in the attack against wired and prepared defences. Whatever the tactical role of the force to which they are allotted, the tanks' part should be offensive action to assist the infantry. Full advantage will not be gained from their characteristics and their special qualities in attack if

employed in a static role and they should not be so used except in very exceptional circumstances.

The conditions favouring successful attack by infantry tanks have been laid down in Section 2.

Attack against modern organized defence can only succeed if it strikes a violent and concentrated blow. It is essential, therefore, that the attacker should exploit to the utmost those assets he can command, such as his ability to choose the time and place of attack and his ability to concentrate his troops.

In the execution of his attack he can best defeat the defence by pushing in with the greatest rapidity compatible with the effective co-operation of all arms. The components of the attack should fall upon the defence in rapid succession; the artillery covering fire should be closely followed by tanks which, in their turn, should be closely followed by the infantry.

The susceptibility of the tank to ground makes it important that the area selected for the attack should provide suitable ground for the employment of tanks. Besides the qualities of good firm going and defilade enumerated in Section 2, the ground should provide cover for assembly and approach of the tanks. Open country is desirable as woods, villages and enclosed country are not favourable for tank action.

2. *A co-ordinated plan.*—To ensure success it is necessary to allow sufficient time for preparation of a timed and co-ordinated plan and for junior commanders, if possible down to crew commanders, to reconnoitre and effect liaison with the attacking infantry.

For the normal use of infantry tanks, against strong defences, the plan will include the provision of adequate artillery support for the attack. A formation commander planning an attack will deal only with one Infantry tank commander. The latter, after reconnaissance, must be prepared to advise on the suitability of various sectors for tank action, and on the extent of front that can be attacked by the tank units under his command.

Situations may arise, however, in which co-ordinated attack must be mounted in a limited time, e.g., in the stage of exploitation after a "break-in". All commanders in infantry tank units must, therefore, be trained in rapidity in reconnaissance and in preparing a co-ordinated plan of attack. The procedure detailed in Part II is designed to simplify and speed up this process. It must be a point of honour that the infantry tank preparations shall not be the "limiting factor" in the time needed by a commander to launch his attack.

It is most desirable that tanks and infantry should attack on the same axis. The convergent attack is possible provided a proportion of tank support is available on the same axis as the infantry attack. The difficulties of timing and the provision of fire support are however great.

3. *Use in mass.*—For a planned attack on prepared defences with a modern establishment of anti-tank weapons it will seldom be economical to use less than one army tank battalion. Usually it will be essential to use more. Tanks should be concentrated against the decisive sector of the objective.

4. *Surprise.*—To gain surprise it will generally be necessary to move tanks under cover of darkness to conceal concentration areas within reach of the sector of attack and to move forward to the starting line from these areas at the last possible moment.

5. *Timing the attack.*—The success of an attack supported by infantry tanks depends very largely on an accurately timed plan. Infantry tanks can advance straight across good going in good light as fast as 200 yards a minute. They will need to manoeuvre to seek out machine guns and to make the best use of ground to avoid the fire of anti-tank guns. Over difficult going this may reduce their general rate of advance as low as 50 yards a minute. The tank commander must be able accurately to estimate what will be the rate of advance of the tanks over the successive stages of the advance.

The covering fire of the attack must start when the attacking tanks come under observation by the enemy.

The artillery supporting fire will then lift forward on a time programme based on the tank commander's estimate of his rate of advance. To this programme tank commanders must then, throughout, adjust their movements while carrying out their role and ensuring cohesion with the following Infantry:—

The attack will be made in bounds—the infantry will as a rule cross the starting line in accordance with a timed programme.

Where the rate of advance of the tanks is high it will be necessary to arrange for pauses on the various bounds to allow the attacking infantry to close up.

6. *Artillery support.*—As a general rule the artillery support should be directed to cover the advance of the tanks, the latter being responsible for dealing with the hostile small arms fire which is stopping the advancing infantry.

As hostile anti-tank guns are unlikely to have disclosed their position until the tanks appear, concentrations are unlikely to be effective and a barrage will be necessary. In suitable weather conditions some saving in the intensity of the barrage may be effected by the use of smoke. It must be remembered, however, that in adverse weather conditions, smoke may be a greater enemy than friend to attacking tanks by providing a background against which they are clearly silhouetted. Tanks then become an easy mark to the hostile anti-tank gunner.

Pauses on bounds will require the protection of covering fire unless adequate natural cover for the tanks is available. In suitable conditions smoke may be employed.

A smoke screen on an undefiladed flank of the tank attack can usually be made to provide a considerable degree of protection against anti-tank guns engaging the tanks from outside the flank of the area of attack.

The successful use of smoke is entirely dependent upon weather conditions which cannot be accurately foretold and are subject to sudden change. All fire plans which include smoke must have an alternative programme. The artillery commander is responsible for early notification to all concerned when a change of plan of necessary.

F.O.Os. in armoured O.Ps. will move well forward to direct artillery fire on to unexpected resistance, and some guns will be at the call of F.O.Os. for this purpose. The tank commander must know the number of F.O.Os. provided, their orders and the number of guns controlled by each.

7. *Small arms support.*—Small arms support is provided by:—
    Medium machine guns.
    Light machine guns.
    3-inch Mortars.
    Platoon weapons.

The main functions of all these weapons are:—
    The neutralization of anti-tank weapons during the attack.
    The consolidation of the position on capture.

Some of these will be used to provide the initial supporting fire for the attack and some to accompany it.

Supporting fire will normally be provided by heavy machine guns from stationary positions. These weapons can continue to fire later than the artillery as their fire will not damage the tanks. The accompanying weapons are required to engage targets of opportunity which have escaped the supporting programme and to protect the flanks. Anti-tank guns should be dealt with by lethal weapons rather than smoke.

Carriers may be usefully employed to get light machine guns forward to provide such fire.

The occupation and consolidation of the position is the duty of the infantry. Carriers may at times be used to transport light machine guns quickly on to the position which they will occupy dismounted.

8. *The tank advance.*—The attacking tanks must be deployed as near the infantry start line as possible.

Suitable formations for advance are considered below (Secs. 7, 3 and 8, 2). The formation must be dense enough to enable the tanks to search the ground thoroughly yet open enough to allow of sufficient room for minor manoeuvre against anti-tank guns. There must be sufficient depth to ensure that enemy machine guns, missed through casualties or change of direction of leading tanks, are dealt with by following tanks: there must also be local reserves of tanks.

As the defence will generally be protected by wire entanglements, the density of tanks is also influenced by the necessity of making sufficient breaches in the wire for the infantry.

In an advance against organized defences, the first echelon precedes the infantry. Its task is:—

(i) To fall upon the enemy on the frontage of attack before he has time to recover from the fire of supporting weapons.

(ii) To neutralize the automatic weapons in its zone of action in order to allow the infantry to advance.

In consequence, this echelon must have sufficient depth to enable these tasks to be carried out and to allow of mutual support between sections both laterally and in depth.

The leading sections must close with the enemy before he has time to recover from the action of the artillery. The rearmost sections must regulate their pace to that of the infantry and endeavour to neutralize all enemy small arms fire left by the leading sections.

The second echelon should move normally in rear of the advancing infantry. They must be prepared to move at once in front or to the flank of the infantry in order to deal with any short range small arms fire causing checks to the latter.

Against unorganized resistance and in certain types of ground favourable to an infantry advance but unfavourable to tanks, the first echelon of tanks may follow the leading infantry. In this case their role will be similar to that of the second echelon tanks employed against organized resistance.

The battalion commander will retain a local reserve for use against the unexpected, maintenance of momentum and the use of local exploitation of success.

Woods and villages present special difficulties. Tanks are unable to neutralize enemy who take refuge in buildings or in thick cover and are themselves vulnerable to anti-tank weapons at short range. They therefore operate under severe disadvantages.

Such localities are, however, easily identified on the ground and on the map and, if not too large, provide targets which can be dealt with comparatively easily by artillery fire and this should be the normal means of neutralizing the fire of their defenders.

Experience proves that a defender often clings stoutly to localities of this kind, however intense the artillery covering fire, and that the attacking infantry will be held up until assistance of close supporting weapons or tanks is forthcoming.

Tanks should not pass enclosed localities until they are certain that fire from them is not holding up the infantry advance. If strongly held it may be necessary for tanks to deal with them to enable the infantry to effect a footing. The first essential is to neutralize the enemy fire coming from the edge of the enclosure.

9. *The infantry advance.*—In selecting the infantry start line and the formation in which leading infantry are formed up before the start it must be remembered that hostile defensive fire is certain to come down as soon as the enemy hears or sees the tanks or when the supporting artillery fire begins.

The infantry should as a rule advance as close behind the leading tanks as it is possible for them to do. The closer they can keep the safer for both arms as they will be able to tackle the machine gun which has gone to ground to avoid the tank before it has been able to come to life again, and to assist the tanks by bringing fire to bear on hostile anti-tank guns which have not been effectively neutralized by the artillery.

10. *Action on the objective.*—Tanks, on arrival on the objective, will patrol their sectors to neutralize enemy weapons. In some cases the presence of tanks on the objective will be sufficient to enable the infantry to secure it. Tanks must, however, always be prepared to deal with areas beyond or to the flank of the

objective if such action is necessary to assist the infantry. Patrols will be carried out so as to keep the tanks as far as possible "hull down" to enemy weapons beyond the objective. They will then hoist the all clear signal. They must not be left alone on the objective longer than necessary as this involves the danger of the enemy destroying them by artillery fire or by anti-tank guns moving forward, with a consequent risk of the enemy re-establishing themselves on the objective.

Liaison beforehand should have arranged a point where the senior tank company or section commander on the objective will meet the infantry battalion or company commander and ascertain that the infantry are up and that tanks can rally.

Tanks will in the first instance rally by sections under cover, if possible just in rear of the captured position. If the attack is to proceed to a further objective, they will deploy to resume the attack from these forward rallying points. On the final objective they will rally well back once the infantry notify that they are organized against counter-attack by both enemy infantry and A.F.Vs.

11. *Maintenance of the momentum of the attack.*—Once the organized resistance of the enemy is broken and the timed artillery programme has ended, the further progress of this attack will depend on the initiative of forward units or sub-unit commanders.

With tanks available it may be possible to achieve considerable success by means of rapidly mounted local attacks to defeat enemy elements still holding out.

In these circumstances decentralization will produce the quickest results and tank company commanders should operate under the orders of leading infantry unit commanders at this stage when speed and initiative are essential to success.

Section 6. The Battalion in Attack

1. *Role of the battalion commander.*—An army tank unit may be either "under command" or "in support" of a formation.

In the former case the formation commander will make the plan and has the whole tank unit at his disposal. In the latter case the plan is made by higher formation and the disposal of the tanks is decided by this formation.

Before action, in addition to ensuring that his unit is ready for action, the battalion commander will ensure that he is always in possession of all available information concerning possible plans and sectors of attack and that his officers are kept similarly informed as far as is necessary.

In action he will accompany his unit, reporting progress by R./T. to the commander under whose orders he is operating, being ready to control the action of his battalion reserve as necessary.

2. *Liaison.*—When it appears probable that the battalion will be employed, the battalion commander will send a liaison officer to join the headquarters of the formation with which the battalion is operating. The officer must be of sufficient rank and experience to fully represent his commanding officer with the formation to which he is attached.

On arrival at the formation headquarters the liaison officer will report to the formation signal officer and arrange for the placing of the anchor R./T. set.

His duties while at formation headquarters are:—

(i) To act as a connecting link for the transmission of information and orders;

(ii) To keep in touch with the intentions of the formation commander and with the latest information regarding ground, enemy defences and any anti-tank mine fields known to be laid by our own or enemy troops;

(iii) To assist his commanding officer in suggesting anticipatory reconnaissance or moves. For this purpose he must know any traffic arrangements in force and the general layout of artillery and signal cables so as to avoid damaging them.

(iv) To accompany his commanding officer when he is called to conference and to take notes. He should at such times meet him on his arrival at headquarters with an up-to-date situation map.

(v) In the absence of his commanding officer, to assist with technical advice if asked.

(vi) During battle to "listen in" to the battalion link-set and pass important information therefrom to the general staff; such information from tank units will often be the first news of the progress of the attack received at formation headquarters.

(vii) He should not leave formation headquarters without reporting to the general staff and satisfying himself that signals know the location of his battalion. He must arrange reliefs and food for personnel accompanying him.

The proper execution of these duties requires alertness and tact. The liaison officer must cultivate the art of seeing and hearing without annoying busy staff officers.

3. *The battalion plan.*—The most responsible duty of the battalion commander in the field is to assist the formation commander in planning the attack.

He will advise on the most suitable sector for the action of his battalion, the frontage of attack, the timing of artillery support and co-ordination with infantry attack.

Frontages.—As a guide in open country and with reasonable visibility, an army tank battalion is able to neutralize the frontage which can be attacked by an infantry battalion.

Where successive objectives are to be attacked he should urge a relatively smaller frontage to enable him to act with a reserve.

4. *Handling of the battalion reserve.*—The objects of the battalion reserve are:—

(i) To deal with eventualities which may prevent the commander's plan from being fulfilled. In particular to deal with counter-attack by defending tanks.

(ii) To relive forward companies and maintain the momentum of the attack.

(iii) To overcome opposition not dealt with by the forward companies in their advance.

In timing the movements of the reserve it is necessary to strike a compromise between being so close to the leading companies that it is not possible to manoeuvre freely when a new situation arises, and being so far in rear that the leading companies are liable to defeat in detail.

5. *Leap frogging.*—In the original orders for an attack, arrangements for the relief of forward companies should usually correspond with reliefs of infantry battalions or brigades so as to facilitate liaison. Heavy casualties or the intervention of hostile tanks may, however, make it necessary to relieve forward companies at a stage not provided for in orders, and R./T. control makes it possible to alter the dispositions of a tank battalion at any stage in the attack.

6. *Rallying.*—The battalion commander will lay down the general policy for forward rallying areas. He will also lay down a rear rallying area for the whole battalion on completion of the attack.

During a prolonged action it may be necessary to replenish with ammunition in forward rallying areas. Normally all replenishment and maintenance is carried out in the rear rallying area.

Section 7. The Company in the Attack

1. *A company in support of a formation.*—A tank company is normally allotted "in support of" an infantry formation or unit, the orders for the attack being issued by the tank battalion commander. The company commander will,

however, establish early liaison with the infantry commander concerned and should ascertain from him the areas or localities to which he attaches especial importance.

In exceptional circumstances a tank company may be placed under command of an infantry brigade or battalion. Such circumstances may arise in the case of a minor operation, or when the organized resistance of the enemy has been broken. The tank company commander will keep in touch with the tank battalion commander by R./T. so that he may receive orders relating to re-centralization of command and for the passage of information.

2. *Liaison with infantry commander.*—Whether "in support of" or "under command", a tank company commander will take the first opportunity of getting into touch with the commander of the infantry he is supporting and will not leave a forward rallying area without reporting to the infantry commander.

3. *Formations.*—The details of formations are given in Part II. As few tanks as can be expected to deal with the enemy's defensive organization on the frontage should be used ahead of infantry, and as many as possible retained in second echelon for action against the unexpected.

4. *Action on the objective.*—Tank company commanders should get into personal touch with the leading infantry commanders on each objective to plan the details of the advance during the further steps of the attack.

5. *Company reconnaissance officer.*—In action this officer will also act as company liaison officer. His resources for communication are confined to D.R. or light tank.

His most important duty in this connection is to convey to his company commander alterations in orders and dispositions which have been made after the tank company commander has left infantry headquarters.

He should accompany the infantry commander with whom his company is co-operating during the battle as closely as his means of transport permit and should assist the infantry commander in maintaining communication with his company commander.

6. *Rallying.*—Company commanders will lay down in orders the general forward rallying areas for sections.

As soon as companies have rallied they will report by R./T. or by light tank to the tank battalion commander stating the results of their attack, and casualties.

Section 8. The Section in Attack

1. *General.*—The section commander is responsible for controlling the movements of his section in such a way as to fulfil the intentions of his commander and to ensure that all enemy within the zone allotted to him are dealt with effectively.

He should be ready to direct his section to a flank to deal with opposition outside his immediate objective or to the rear to deal with opposition which has re-emerged from cover.

The section commander should avoid his own tank becoming closely engaged in the early stages of an attack. He should confine himself to controlling his tanks, treating his own tank as a section reserve to deal with emergencies.

2. *Formations.*

Line or three up.	Enables an exposed space to be crossed in the shortest time.
Line ahead.	A march formation, may be necessary for the passage of a defile.
One up.	One up with section commander leading.
Two up.	Two up with section commander in rear.
	These two latter are variations of line; the section commander moves where he can best command. They give depth and therefore control, and allow the best use to be made of ground.

3. *Action during early stages of the attack.*—During the early stages of the attack before the enemy's forward defended localities are reached, sections should be led so as to take every advantage of cover and so close with the enemy with minimum loss.

The use of covered approaches should not however lead section commanders to neglect the searching of ground which may contain enemy. The risk of deploying from a narrow approach under the short range fire of field guns or anti-tank weapons should also be considered.

4. *Buildings and enclosures.*—In the course of the attack small enclosures, woods and buildings in which an enemy can take cover from tanks will be encountered for which no provision has been made in orders. Sections which encounter such localities should keep them under fire and should not leave until the infantry have entered them.

5. *Clearing crests.*—Crests should be crossed in line with guns bearing forward.

Whenever possible section commanders should examine from cover or from a hull down position open ground over which he may have to lead his section with a view to the selection of the most covered routes for his tanks.

6. *Direct liaison with infantry.*—During an attack it is sometimes necessary for section commanders or crew commanders to communicate directly with infantry commanders. They should be ready to halt their tanks on receiving the intercommunication signal from infantry commanders and should speak through the turret or dismount. Tanks should not, however, be halted in the open exposed to the direct fire of guns.

7. *The tank in the attack.*—The crew commander is responsible for:—

(i) the course taken by the tank which involves attention to the signals of the section commander;

(ii) control of fire which involves the search for targets and attention to enemy movements;

(iii) close co-operation with the attacking infantry which requires constant observation of their progress.

The driver is responsible, without orders, for keeping station and course in the formation ordered. He should, on his own responsibility make minor deviations to avoid natural obstacles and to take advantage of cover. He should be skilled in running his tank up to a position of observation with a minimum of orders for minor readjustments. He should at all times in action drive so as to give his gunner the best chance of using his weapon.

At the same time he should know how to make a difficult target of his tank for enemy gunners by alteration of speed and direction.

Section 9. Defence and Rear Guard

1. *General.*—The primary role of infantry tanks in defence is counter-attack.

As surprise is one of the most important features of a counter-attack, it is of the greatest importance that tanks should remain concealed until the delivery of the attack. The disposition of tanks will depend on the type of counter-attack. This is further discussed below.

The mobility and armament of infantry tanks eminently suit them for employment against A.F.Vs. They will therefore often be held in reserve for action against attacking tanks whether the latter are working in close co-operation with infantry or in a more independent role.

2. *Immediate counter-attack.*—The employment of tanks for immediate counter-attack in forward areas usually involves dispersion and the risk of loss from enemy fire. It will be justified where it has been decided that the loss of a particular portion of the forward defences will seriously jeopardize the plan of the defence and that an immediate counter-attack is likely to present the best chance of regaining it.

The main essentials for immediate counter-attack are:—

(i) Speed. An immediate counter-attack has little chance of success unless it takes place before the enemy has time to consolidate.

(ii) A cut and dried plan which can be put into execution by all the troops concerned at the shortest notice.

(iii) Good arrangements for continuous liaison between the infantry and tank commanders.

(iv) A limited objective.

Tanks may be employed in immediate counter-attack against hostile tanks which have outrun their infantry. This is further dealt with in Section 10.

3. *Deliberate counter-attack.*—This is carried out with the object of regaining lost ground and is executed on the same principles as other attacks by the co-ordinated effort of infantry, artillery and tanks.

4. *Organization of defensive area.*—The whole area must be thoroughly reconnoitred by tank commanders who may be called upon to operate over it.

The advantage of detailed reconnaissance of ground enjoyed by the defenders must be exploited to the full and special maps prepared showing tank obstacles, minefields within our defensive system and passages through them.

Crossing places and channels of movement over obstacles must be prepared and marked for the use of defending tanks.

Section 10. Tank v. Tank

1. *General.*—Although the action of opposing forces both capable of simultaneous fire and movement is comparatively new in land warfare, it must not be thought that the familiar principles of war cease to apply.

The commonsense application of the following principles of land warfare will be found to produce the best results:—

(i) Before manoeuvre can be attempted the enemy must be pinned, or at any rate the freedom of his manoeuvre restricted. This is best effected by the fire of anti-tank guns and artillery, by natural or artificial obstacles and lastly by the fire of tanks from concealed positions.

(ii) The bulk of the available tank force should be utilized for manoeuvre in a direction which will force the enemy tank commander to abandon his object.

2. *Armament.*—Tank v. tank tactics depend to a great extent on the armament, armour and speed of the opposing vehicles.

The infantry tank is immune against the weapons carried by light tanks. The latter will, however, often be able to avoid action with infantry tanks by using their superior speed.

Tanks shooting from a stationary concealed position enjoy a considerable advantage over tanks on the move.

3. *Action against hostile tanks.*—If the action of hostile tanks is preventing the attacking tanks from attaining their object of getting the infantry forward, the attacking tanks must take action to destroy or drive away the defending tanks.

Against defending tanks which are skilfully handled the leading sections will often be caught at a disadvantage. They should, however, endeavour to engage the enemy's fire and attention. If possible they should themselves seek cover from which they can engage the enemy hull down. The reserve sections should manoeuvre against the flank and rear of the enemy and drive them from cover.

The battalion reserve may in its turn be called upon to operate against the enemy tanks, or if the latter have been driven off by the leading companies he may support the infantry in their advance.

The presence of hostile tanks imposes a great responsibility on the Battalion Commander who should endeavour to control the action of his battalion as long as possible and re-constitute a reserve with which to resume his original task.

GERMAN PANZER TACTICS

One of the clauses of the Treaty of Versailles banned Germany from manufacturing or importing tanks or armoured cars. However, as tanks were considered likely to be useful for the future development of the armed forces, German industry was covertly encouraged to look at tank design. In 1921, an arrangement with the Soviet Union meant that tanks could be secretly developed and tested on Soviet soil, and later a secret school for tank commanders was established at Kazan.

One of the pioneers of German tank theory was an officer of the clandestine German General Staff, Heinz Guderian, whose study of tank tactics led to his proposing a strategic tank force as early as 1929. Tanks were not to be used in infantry divisions, but in independent panzer divisions. In 1931 Colonel Oswald Lutz became Inspector of Motor Transport Troops and Guderian became his Chief of Staff. Lutz oversaw the motorisation of the army, while Guderian created the armoured forces.

Guderian's strategy was for the large-scale concentrated use of the tank, using its speed and mobility to outflank and encircle the enemy. The armoured troops were the decisive offensive weapon, at the spearhead of the offensive. Panzers were vulnerable to infantry and artillery, so the panzer divisions would provide all the support and protection the tanks needed to succeed, this would eventually evolve to include motorised infantry, artillery, engineers, signals and anti-aircraft troops. Strategy and tactics emphasised speed, the massed use of tanks, and the importance of surprise. Coordinating large-scale hard-hitting attacks was possible because of a focus on detailed planning, good communications, and the thorough training of tank commanders.

Not everyone agreed with Guderian's ideas but Hitler's support after he came to power in 1933 assured the rapid expansion of the panzer forces. Panzer divisions were organised in many different ways and as the war progressed combat-ready tanks and supporting troops might be also assembled into *kampfgruppen*.

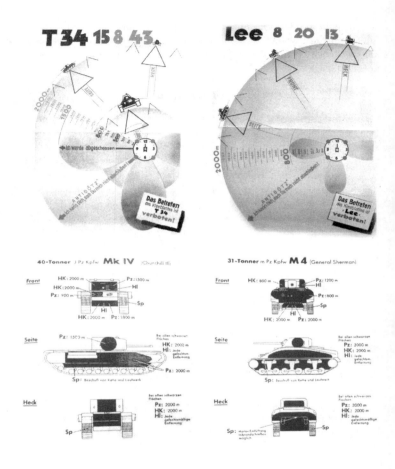

The *Tigerfibel* (*Tiger primer*) was markedly different from most German military manuals and regulations, using amusing and saucy cartoons and rhymes to instruct crews. Its success meant that a similar manual was developed for the Panther, the *Pantherfibel* in 1943. Fold out supplements in the back provided recognition data on enemy tanks, and graphic representations of what range the Tiger could penetrate the armour of enemy tanks, and at what range it could be penetrated.

The following extract comes from the 1940 edition of Friedrich von Cochenhausen's *Taktisches Handbuch für den Truppenführer und seinen Gehilfen* (*Tactical Handbook for the Troop Commander and his Assistants*). Popular when first published in 1923, it went through a series of editions; this 13th edition took into account the early lessons of the war. While not official it was authoritative and was still used, particularly by junior officers and officer candidates, in 1942, when this extract was translated for the American *Tactical and Technical Trends*.

Tactical Handbook for the Troop Commander

1. Preparation for the attack

a. <u>General</u>. The time before an attack should be spent in studying the terrain, preparing positions, and making arrangements to work with the other arms. The study of the terrain should cover the area from the assembly position forward to the front line, and then as far as possible into the enemy's position. The tank force commander, or an officer chosen by him, should take part in this study. Aerial photographs should be used along with the map. It is important to find out the location of mines and the position of the enemy's defense weapons.

b. <u>Surprise</u>. Surprise is most important for a successful attack. Therefore, all preparations must be carefully camouflaged. Tank units should be moved at night, and in the daytime they should move only when they can be hidden from enemy airplanes. The time of the tank attack must be set so that it will come as a surprise. The enemy can be kept from knowing that an attack is coming by engaging him in a few local actions, as well as by camouflaging our radio communications or by keeping the radio silent.

c. <u>Organization of the Tank Force</u>. The tank force commander must decide in every case whether he is going to attack with his tanks in line or in column. An attack in column facilitates control, and makes it possible to maneuver tanks in any direction; to attack in line makes the enemy stretch out his defense, and supports the infantry attack over a broader front.

d. <u>Objectives</u>. Tanks set out to attack the enemy's infantry and infantry heavy weapons, artillery, command posts, reserves and rear communications. But before they can get through to these targets, they must destroy their most dangerous enemy, the antitank defenses. For this reason the heaviest and most powerful tanks must lead the attack, and they must be supported by the other arms, both before and during an attack.

Only after the antitank defenses have been destroyed can the tanks go ahead. After that, the most powerful tanks should be directed to attack the points that are deepest within the enemy positions, such as artillery, reserves, and command posts. The lighter tanks attack the infantry. Each echelon of tanks should be definitely informed concerning its mission and its objectives.

Tank forces are also able to seize important points, such as river crossings, and to hold them until the infantry comes up.

e. Assembly positions. The Panzer division usually prepares for an attack in a position, not too near the battlefield, which gives cover against observation and is beyond the range of the enemy artillery. Here the troops should be told what they are to do, supplies should be distributed, and fuel and ammunition issued. If the tank force by itself cannot protect the position, the commander should see to it that the necessary supporting weapons are brought up.

The tanks can go to the attack more quickly if there are several roads leading from the position to the front, and if crossings over railroads, highways, and rivers have been constructed by engineers.

When time is the most important factor, tank units should remain in their assembly positions for a limited period, or they should move directly to the attack without stopping in these positions.

2. Support of the Tank Attack by Other Troops

a. Infantry. The infantry must direct its heavy machine guns against the enemy's antitank defenses. The other heavy weapons must fire at targets outside the area of the tank action so that they will not disable their own tanks. Signals must be arranged in advance (such as tracers, flags, and radios) so that coordination is assured.

b. Artillery. The artillery fires upon targets in front and to the flanks of the area of the tank action. It fires both high explosives and smoke, and must generally regulate its fire by time. Adjustment can be attained through the radio or the artillery liaison detail, which, riding in armored vehicles, can accompany the tanks.

c. <u>Engineers</u>. Engineers assist the tanks by strengthening bridges, building temporary crossings, and removing obstacles and mines.

d. <u>Signal Troops</u>. Signal troops keep up communications with the commanders, with the artillery, with the services, and with separate units of infantry, engineers, or the air force.

e. <u>Antitank Units</u>. Antitank guns must follow the tanks as closely as possible so as to able to enter the fight immediately if enemy tanks are met.

f. <u>Aviation</u>. Aviation has two duties: it should serve as reconnaissance before and during the time the tanks are in action, and it should attack the enemy's reserves, especially tanks and antitank defenses, before they can come into action.

g. <u>Rear Services</u>. If a tank force does not have its own medical service, it should be kept in touch with first-aid stations of the assisting troops. During the battle the service troops are held in readiness well to the rear.

h. As soon as the tanks reach their objectives, they at once prepare themselves for a new mission. They send reconnaissance to the front and find out how far the infantry has advanced. They decide their next movement on the basis of these findings.

i. After the battle the tank force is withdrawn behind the lines and reorganized. The longer it has been in action, the longer the rest period should be.

3. Examples of Combat Orders and Operations

a. <u>General</u>. Orders to the tank force must be brief and simple in all situations during a war of movement. It is enough if they tell: (1) the location and strength of the enemy; (2) the location and mission of our own troops; (3) the mission for the tank force, to include direction of attack, the objective, and sometimes the hour the tanks are to attack and their action after the attack; and (4) what support is to be given by other arms.

b. Example No.1 (see figure No.1) illustrates an order to a Panzer detachment in the advance.
(1) <u>The Order</u>. The Motorcycle Battalion has encountered the enemy and has deployed on each side of the road in front of Hill 304.

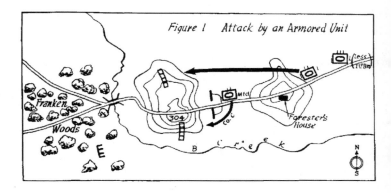

Figure 1   Attack by an Armored Unit

The commander of the 1st Battalion, 1st Panzer Regiment, meets the commander of the advance guard (probably the motorcycle battalion commander) at the forester's house. After receiving brief information about the terrain, he issues the following order:

"The enemy holds Hill 304. Hostile artillery, estimated to be one battery, is firing from the direction south of Franken Woods.

"The Motorcycle Battalion deploys for attack on both sides of the road. Company C is advancing here left of the road against the southern edge of Hill 304.

"The 1st Battalion, moving north of the road, will attack Hill 304. After overcoming the resistance thereon, it will continue across B Creek to attack the enemy artillery south of Franken Woods. It will continue combat reconnaissance to the far end of Franken Woods. I want to know:
a. When the crossing over B Creek begins.
b. When the hostile artillery has been reached and overcome."

(2) The Engagement. The commander of the 1st Battalion then drives to the commander of Company A and orders him to advance around the northern edge of the woods just in front of him and to attack Hill 304. He then gives the necessary commands to the other companies by radio.

While Company A is deploying, Company B, with its left flank on the road, advances against Hill 304. Company D supports the attack from the vicinity of the forester's house. Company C, forming the second line, follows Companies A and B, and the Battalion commander advances with it. As soon as Company A reaches Hill 304, Company D begins to displace forward to this position.

Meantime, the artillery has been definitely located south of Franken Woods. The Battalion commander now issues a new order to attack the artillery, and Companies A, B and D proceed around Hill 304. Company C then engages the remaining resistance on Hill 304 until the motorcyclists come up from the south side. A part of Company A carries out the reconnaissance on the far side of Franken Woods.

c. <u>Attack Against a Prepared Position</u>. If the tanks are to attack a prepared defensive position, the commander of the force must then coordinate all the arms in his command to assist the tanks. Therefore, every arm must be told exactly what to do in an action which is intended first of all to support the tanks against the enemy's antitank weapons.

(1) <u>Preparation</u>. The commander tells the tank force commander about such matters as the enemy, the terrain, and the plan of attack. The tank force commander reports the results of his own reconnaissance, how he thinks the attack should be carried out, and what sort of support he wants. The commander then makes his decision and draws up the order. The tank force commander then informs his subordinates about the terrain and what he intends to do. The tank forces advance to the assembly position on the roads that the commander has assigned to them. These roads are kept free to other troops.

(2) <u>The Tank Force Combat Order</u>. The order should contain:

(a) Information about the enemy (his position, strength, and the location of known and suspected antitank weapons) and the position of our troops. All later messages from the front that contain information for the tanks are passed on at once to the tank force commander.

(b) Our own intentions, stated thus:

"Tank force — in —, echelons — at (time) crosses the front line, attacks with the first echelon across —, toward —, advancing thence to —. The second echelon attacks —. After the attack the tanks will —. (This order should give the mission and support furnished by the infantry, if a part of the tank force is not placed directly under an infantry unit or attached to it.)

(c) Artillery —. Smoke —.

(d) Engineers —.

(e) Aviation —.

(f) Signal Communications —.

(g) Rear Services —.

(h) Command post of the higher commander is at — (where reports are to be sent).

d. Example No. 2 (see Figure No. 2) illustrates a typical problem for the cooperation of tanks with other arms.

(1) <u>Situation</u>. An infantry division, encountering increasing hostile resistance, arrived at the line X – X at 1600 hours. The division, supported by the Panzer Brigade, will renew the attack the next morning.

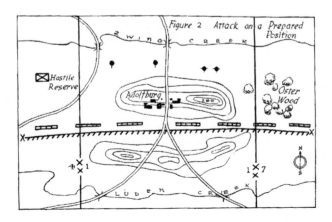

Figure 2   Attack on a Prepared Position

(2) <u>Operations</u>. In the morning, after a brief artillery bombardment, the widely deployed tanks break into the enemy line. The infantry push through the break. Meantime, the artillery advances its fire to the village, Adolfburg, and the Zwing Creek crossings. Smoke troops place fire on the western edge of Oster Wood. Wherever the enemy's antitank weapons are found, they are immediately engaged by heavy infantry weapons and by the tanks. Heavy artillery fire is kept up on Adolfburg. The first echelon of tanks is now advancing rapidly north around both sides of the village; the second echelon decreases its speed and attacks the enemy forces still resisting on the high ground on both sides of Adolfburg. The artillery constantly moves its fire forward so as not to hinder the advancing tanks, being informed by its own forward observers who advance with the leading tanks.

On the right, the infantry attack in the direction of Oster Wood has been checked. Guided to the place by tracers and flag signals, the second echelon of tanks moves towards Oster Wood. Meantime the commander of the first echelon reports:

"Have overcome hostile artillery groups north of Adolfburg. Am continuing towards the artillery discovered farther west. Reconnaissance toward Zwing Creek reports that the stream is passable."

The supporting infantry has been mopping up Adolfburg and the high ground on both sides of the town. This infantry now proceeds to assist the tanks at Oster Wood. Then the heavy weapons and artillery are brought forward to Adolfburg. The enemy, retreating along the road, offers stubborn resistance, but is overcome by elements of the tank battalion cooperating with the advance infantry. Zwing Creek crossings are kept under the fire of tanks, artillery, and combat aviation.

This order was issued by General der Panzertruppen Gustav von Vaerst soon after he became commander of 5. Panzer-Armee, which was fighting in North Africa as part of Heeresgruppe Afrika. It gives a succinct summary of how panzers should be employed. The 5. Panzer-Armee capitulated on 13 May. Translations of this order were then published by both the War Office and by the US War Department later in 1943. A comment followed the translation in the British *Notes from Theatres of War*: 'It will be realized from this document that the German principles of employing tanks show marked differences from our own doctrine of the employment either of infantry tactics or armoured divisions. There have, however, been occasions when the enemy has not applied his own principles in practice. For instance, there have been several reports of tanks accompanying infantry in the attack.'

General Order No. 14

Principles of the employment of tanks

One. The tank is a decisive weapon. It should not be used, therefore, except at the point selected for the main effort, and on suitable terrain.

Two. The tank is not a lone fighter. The smallest tank unit is the troop and, for tasks of some importance, the squadron.

Three. The tank is not a weapon to accompany infantry. Forcing its way through the enemy, it enables the infantry to follow it closely.

Four. The tank is to take, and mop up, a sector, but it cannot hold it. The latter is the task of the infantry, assisted by their support weapons, anti-tank guns, and artillery.

Five. The tank is not an artillery weapon which can harass the enemy from one firing position for a long period. The tank fights by movement, and only subjects its targets to fire for a short while.

Six. The task of the infantry is to neutralize enemy anti-tank weapons, and to follow up tank attacks quickly in order to gain the best possible profits from the tactical and moral impact.

Seven. The task of the artillery is to support by its fire the assault of the tanks, to neutralize enemy artillery, and to follow up closely in rear of the tanks in order to gain a decisive effect. The task of the supporting artillery is the protection of the flanks of the attacking tanks by fire which lifts at the pace of the advance.

Eight. The task for the Panzer Grenadiers is to follow up closely the attack of the tanks, so as to be able to intervene immediately should a tank v tank battle develop.

Nine. The task of the engineers is to open up lanes through the minefields, under the protection of the tanks, thus making it possible for the tank attack to regain momentum.

Ten. At night the tank is blind and deaf. Therefore the task of the infantry is to protect it with their weapons.

Von Vaerst
Commander-in-Chief of the 5 Pz Army, 10th March 43

CHAPTER 3: IN THEATRE

For tankers, battles often only lasted a few hours; the vast majority of their time was spent on the move, observing, mounting guard, refuelling, carrying out maintenance, training, camouflaging the tank, and finally, after all else was done, cooking, eating, and resting.

As well as their weapon and protection in battle, the tank was the crew's home and shelter. Crews could be very attached to their tank, referring to it by name, though some crews clearly had a love-hate relationship with their mount. Love or hate, tanks had to be carefully tended. The driver would spend most of his spare time tinkering and checking the engine. Nobody would have begrudged him that, as they were all dependent on the tank's mobility in battle. As it was rather crudely put in rather crudely put in *Instruction Book Driving and Maintenance. Tanks Infantry Matilda I, II, III, IV, V*: 'Remember, if your tank becomes immobile, your troop has lost one-third of its fire power – a stationary object is a much easier target than a moving one – do not, by sheer neglect of your periodical maintenance, murder your pals in your crew. Any person can take a tank into battle, but it takes an experienced driver, one who has maintained his vehicle perfectly, to bring it out. ... Nurse your tank as you would your horse. On reaching the bivouac area feed it with fuel, oil and water ... groom it and lubricate it before you feed and groom yourself – have it always ready to move at a moment's notice.'

Of course the maintenance of a Matilda, or any tank, could not be completed by the driver alone; in the same manual are listed the jobs allocated to each member of the crew. The tank commander had 22 specific checks to be carried out before duty, his crew each had more. The wireless operator would have ensured the wireless was in working order. The gun barrel needed cleaning on a daily basis, which required several men. Throwing a track was a constant worry, so good crews would have checked the tracks whenever they could. Repairs would have been carried out by the crew if at all possible. The tank commander would have recorded and reported on completed maintenance. He would be the one to ensure maintenance was carried out despite bad weather or in difficult conditions, and he kept an eye out for conditions that might cause problems for the tank, for example river crossings could wash the grease out of fittings, and rubber gaskets might perish in the cold, leading to leaks.

This 'short' service manual for the Russian T-34 dates to 1942. It notably does not include the regular maintenance necessary for the tank's weapons, which would have been detailed in the manuals for the individual weapons. Additional checks would be completed after a certain number of miles had been covered or the engine had run for a certain number of hours.

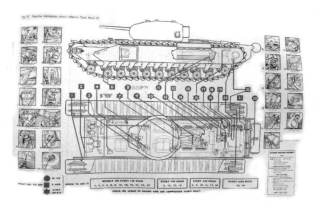

Lubrication chart for a Churchill tank.

T-34 SHORT SERVICE MANUAL

People's Commissariat of Defence of the USSR, Moscow 1942

Chapter VII: MAINTENANCE

The tank must always be in complete fighting readiness. Reliable performance is only possible if the tank is properly maintained. Regular maintenance increases the life of the machine. Tank maintenance consists of:—

1. Filling up with fuel, oil and water.
2. Periodical technical inspection.
3. Periodical lubrication.
4. Systematic checking of the adjustment of assemblies and of the controls.

Filling up

The fuel tanks should be filled with DT Diesel fuel of "Gasoil" mark "3" through a double thickness of silk cloth. If a silk cloth is not available then it is possible to use a flannel with the nap upwards. The funnel must have a mesh filter (mesh size not less than No. 60).

The fuel should be filled into four tanks – 150 litres into the front tanks and 80 litres into the rear tanks and up to the level of the middle ring marked on the filter. The quantity of fuel is measured by a dipstick.

Diesel fuel, summer grade, is suitable for temperatures not less than +5°C and winter grade for use at temperatures of less than +5°C. Winter fuel can be used in summer. At temperatures below -20°C, tractor kerosine should be added to DT winter fuel in the following proportions:—

> from -20 to -30°C – 10% kerosine
> from -30 to -35°C – 25% kerosine
> from -35 to -50°C – 70% kerosine

The fuel can be drained from the drain plugs underneath the tanks. To do this the end of a flexible tube should be screwed on to the threaded plug which should then be unscrewed from 2 to 3 turns.

Oil

The oil tanks are filled with "Avia" oil MK or MS or MZS through the mesh filter (mesh size not being less than No. 60). In winter at temperatures below -20°C it is recommended to fill up with MZS "Avia" oil. Of the oil tanks two of 57 litre capacity each are filled up to 40 litres. The quantity of oil is measured by a dipstick. The minimum permissible quantity of oil in the tanks is 20 litres.

The oil is drained through plugs situated in the base of the tanks. In winter it is recommended to drain off the oil before long halts. In winter the oil should only be filled after the engine has been warmed with water (warmed to 80–90°C) filled into the tanks and 5–6 litres into the engine.

Water

The cooling system is filled with water through the mouth of the filler opening over the engine. Into the mouth of the opening is introduced a funnel with mesh filter. If the steam valve is opened the water can be poured in more quickly.

The system will take 95 litres of water and the level should come to about 2–3 m/m. from the base of the filler mouth.

A tap is fitted to the water pump to drain the water. To do this the hand lever of the tap on the engine bulkhead should be turned to the vertical position.

To clear the pump of water it is necessary to turn the crank shaft round 2–3 turns.

In winter at temperatures lower than -20°C the cooling system should be filled either with anti-freeze or a mixture of glycerine, spirit and water. Anti-freeze expands on heating and therefore the cooling system should be filled with 5–6 litres less than when filling with water.

Sometimes anti-freeze will not flow as at -50°C it is transformed into a porous mass but this does not cause a crack in the system.

Anti-freeze is a costly product and care must be taken to prevent wastage.

TECHNICAL INSPECTION OF THE VEHICLE

External Inspection

1. Inspect the condition of the tracks, track pins and their keepers (split pins). Each track should be hit with a hammer to reveal any cracks.
2. Check the track tension.
3. Test the joint between the idler crank arm and the hull for firmness.
4. Check the lubricator plugs of the suspension for tightness.
5. Inspect the brackets and fixtures of the entrenching tool, spare tracks, jettison tanks, tarpaulin and tool box.

Inspection of Engine and Transmission Compartment

1. Every accessible place should be cleaned with a rag.
2. See that there are no foreign bodies on the floor under the fan.
3. Check the fuel, oil and water systems for correct flow. Test the "durite" hoses for firmness. See that the fuel system is hermetically sealed under 0.2–0.3 m/m.
4. See that the clearance between the brake bands and drums is 1.5–2.0m/m. all round.
5. See that there is no leakage of oil from the gearbox.
6. Test the tie rods and split pins of the control linkages.

Inspection of the Fighting and Driving Compartment

1. Test the locking of the nut of the idler wheel nut.
2. See that the accessories are not on the floor under the control-rods.

3. Test the working of the driving control and see that the ball and socket joints are not disconnected that the levers are not resting on the floor and that the split pins are properly secured.

4. Test the pressure in the air bottles. The maximum pressure is 150 atm. The minimum pressure is 30 atm. in the summer and 65 atm. in winter.

5. Check the position of the hand levers of the drain cock:— horizontal position – cock closed, vertical – open.

6. Check the position of the fuel change-over cock. The hand lever should be pointing downwards – all tanks switched off.

7. Test the quantity of grease in the water pump pressure lubricator.

8. Inspect the earth switch.

9. Check the fire extinguisher.

10. Inspect the working parts of the electrical circuit for damage.

11. Test the horn and lights.

At the outbreak of war the 1st Royal Tank Regiment was part of the Heavy Armoured Brigade in Egypt. The regiment was at Tobruk in the summer of 1941 and El Alamein in October 1942. It would later advance through Italy in 1943, and take part in the Normandy landings. Fighting in the desert offered an additional set of challenges, and caused great fatigue to tank crews, as noted in this British report of 1942:

> The men are wakened at about 0500 hours, that is, before daylight, get into their tanks, and drive out from harbour to battle or patrol positions, which must be reached before first light. Battles commonly occur in the early morning or the late afternoon or evening. In the middle of the day the heat haze is usually so great as to make accurate fire difficult. It is unusual for actual fighting to occupy more than three of the daylight hours, the rest of the time being spent in patrolling and waiting, and preparing, for an attack. Although fighting is not taking place it is not normally possible for crews to get out of their tanks or to cook any meals because of enemy harassing fire. Tank commanders have a particularly tiring time because they have to remain standing in order to keep their head above the turrets, and must constantly be on the alert. Usually about 2100 hours, or later, the opposing tanks gradually draw apart and finally seek their respective harbours. This move may necessitate two or three hours of night

driving on the part of the tank crews in order to reach some suitable point from which to start for the next day's battle. On harbouring, tanks must be refuelled and re-armed, and minor repair and general maintenance carried out. It is rarely before 0100 hours that the men are at last able to get into their blankets. Since, however, each man in turn must stand an hour's guard, three hours' sleep is about the maximum that can be obtained. (Notes from Theatres of War 10)

These undated orders and training notes, compiled during 1 RTR's time in the Western Desert, reflect the lessons taught by long experience of living in the desert and fighting German and Italian forces.

BATTLE STANDING ORDERS AND TRAINING NOTES

1st ROYAL TANK REGIMENT

These Orders and Training Notes are applicable more to warfare in the Western Desert and have been produced to give guidance to all ranks in the methods of command, control, and administration which have been found by experience over a long period of operations to be satisfactory. They are not exhaustive and will require amendment from time to time in light of future experience. However, if they are read and interpreted sensibly, they form a sound basis on which the command and administration of the Regiment is organised. The training notes are a guide both to training prior to action and to the tactical handling of sub-units in action.

Squadron leaders will ensure that all ranks are instructed in and become fully acquainted with the contents of this document. All commanders of sub-units attached to the Regiment will also note such paragraphs as apply to their particular arm.

These orders do not supersede Regimental Standing Orders but amplify them to suit wartime conditions. Regimental Standing Orders, written to apply more to peacetime conditions, should also be studied in conjunction with these Battle Standing Orders and Training Notes.

PART A: OPERATIONS

1. Command and Communications

Command is exercised by the Commanding Officer, or in his absence by the Second in Command, by R/T from his tank or by the issue of verbal or written orders.

(a) In addition to all tanks of the Regiment, the following W/T stations will be maintained on regimental forward control.

O.C. A Echelon

O.C. A1 Echelon (forward replenishment)

The Regiment will be in communication with B Echelon through A Echelon using the Brigade 'Q' frequency.

(b) Whenever possible, in order to conserve batteries, sub-units will be permitted to close down. Sub-units will send a runner to RGQ, and when he has reported, and not before, the order to close down will be given over the air. Relief of runners will be a sub-unit responsibility.

(c) Commanding Officers' Conferences.

The following will normally attend:—

2 i.c.	Adjutant
Sqn Comds	R.T.A.
OC B Ech (if available)	Signals Officer
OC A Ech	I.O.
OC A1 Ech	Navigator

OsC Attached sub-units

The Adjutant will arrange for warning officers as above to attend.

In the event of the C.O. being called to Bde. HQ., No. 1 Party, composed as under, may be called to await his return

2 i.c.

Os.C all sub-units, including attached

Adjutant

OC A Echelon

OC A1 Echelon

I.O.

Navigator

(d) Regimental W/T Net.

The C.Os operator, under the supervision of the Signals Officer, will be responsible for netting the whole forward control group ¼ hour after Reveille daily. Sub-unit commanders will ensure that all operators are on their sets at that time.

(e) Rear Link.

The W/T Rear Link Set to Brigade HQ will be manned by the Adjutant. The 2 i.c. will maintain his set to Brigade HQ on his flick frequency so that he can take over the duties of rear link in the event of the Adjutant's set breaking down. Communication between the C.O. and Rear Link will be B Set.

(f) Relief of Operators.

The provision of relief operators during leaguer is dealt with in Para 4, sub-para 9.

2. Battle Formation

There are normally only two Battle Formations in use in the regt or Regtl Group:—

(a) Air Formation.

This is the normal formation adopted by the Regtl Group at the halt or on the move during any normal march across the open desert or during the approach to contact. At all times in air formations vehicles will be well dispersed, tending to disperse laterally rather than in depth in order to avoid a long tail, except at the halt, when dispersion will be in all directions.

(b) Battle line.

This formation is adopted when the position of the enemy has been established. The two medium squadrons form line facing the enemy either side of and in front of RHQ, taking advantage of the ground in order to get hull down positions. The light squadron will be ordered to one or both flanks and will be prepared to despatch special patrols as ordered by the C.O.

3. March Discipline

A good daily mileage is not made by going fast. This merely causes mechanical breakdown. A good mileage can only be achieved by strict adherence to march discipline.

(a) By Day.

(i) Speed will normally be 10 m.i.h. This is best maintained by an actual speed of not less than 12 m.p.h. by the leading vehicle.

(ii) Dispersion. See para 2 (a) above.

(iii) Halts. Duration of halts will be given over the air and it is the duty of all tank and vehicle commanders to find this out and to be ready to move, with engine running and crew mounted at the termination of the period. A 30 minute halt is the shortest period in which a crew can 'brew' and be ready to move at the correct time.

(iv) When the order to advance is given all vehicles will move off together and will not wait for others to move first. If a vehicle is left behind due to a mechanical fault or other reasons it must make up the distance gradually and not by excessive speed.

(v) Do not use the air unnecessarily. First priority is given to RHQ and the light squadron except when engaged in battle line when the medium squadrons may take precedence. The use of visual signals is normally sufficient during a march.

<u>(b) By Night.</u>

(i) Speed 4 miles in hour varying with the state of the moon.

(ii) The Regimental Group will normally move in night leaguer formation (see Appx. B) and heads of column will keep in visual touch.

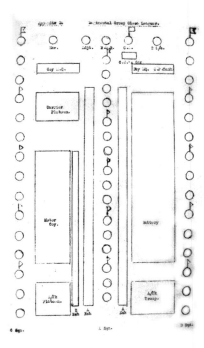

Appendix B: Night Leaguer Formation.

4. Leaguering

<u>(a) By Day.</u>

(i) The Regimental Group will leaguer by day in normal air formation (see Appendix A), facing the enemy or the direction of movement.

(ii) Sub-units may close down W/T sets when they have complied with para. 1 (b) above.

(iii) All guns will be mounted, ready for instant action. Sentries will be posted under sub-unit arrangements.

(iv) Under some circumstances, guard tanks or complete troops may be detailed for local protection.

(v) Sub-unit Commanders and the R.T.A. must be acquainted with the 'Notice to Move' before major maintenance operations are carried out.

(vi) No fires may be lit before sunrise nor may they remain alight after sunset. Fire may be lit before sunrise during winter if permission is given by the C.O.

(vii) All Sanitary arrangements must be made and all food scraps and tins buried, because a leaguer area may be occupied for a long period.

(viii) Slit-trenches will be dug for all B vehicle crews.

(ix) It is the duty of all ranks to know the whereabouts of RHQ and of all and of all sub-unit HQs.

<u>(b) By Night.</u>

(i) Guards are found as follows:—

Double guard on each face armed with T.S.M.Gs. They are found:— on front face from 'A' Echelon, on flanks from medium Squadrons and on the rear face from the Bty. A Guard Commander will be detailed from each of these sub-units to ensure that sentries are changed. Two Orderly Officers will be detailed by the Adjutant nightly to supervise the system. The total guard will therefore consist of 2 Officers 4 N.C.Os and 24 O.Rs. In addition to the above the Motor Coy. will provide a prowler guard for the interior of the leaguer.

(ii) Duties of Guard.

A. Sentries. Each sentry is responsible for half of his face of the leaguer. From a position at least twenty yards from the leaguer he looks and listens for any suspicious movements by vehicles or by men. Anyone approaching the leaguer will be challenged and engaged with fire if the challenge is not answered. The following will immediately be reported to the Guard Commander:— movement of vehicles towards or near the leaguer, movement of men near the leaguer, dropping of flares near or over the leaguer, any other circumstances which may endanger the leaguer. The sentries are responsible that the leaguer is roused punctually at reveille.

B. Guard Commander. He is responsible that the sentries are changed at the correct time and aware of their duties. If the Guard Commander has been roused by a sentry who has given the alarm, he will, if he considers the situation dangerous wake his sub-unit. In order that maximum rest may be obtained this will not be done unless absolutely necessary and the Guard Commander may on occasions ask the advice of his sub-unit commander.

C. Orderly Officer. The Orderly Officer will ensure that the system of sentries and reliefs is correctly carried out. He will visit the sentries at various times to ensure that they are always alert. He will find out what vehicles or parties of vehicles are due to enter the leaguer during the night and will warn the sentries. He will make certain that vehicles entering the leaguer during the night are directed to their correct position so as not to disturb the leaguer. He will ensure that no naked lights are shown, that all ranks go to bed as soon as possible after they have completed their duties and there is no unnecessary talking or noise. He will be in possession of a verey pistol, coloured lights, and the ground to air recognition signals of the day.

(iii) Under normal circumstances, reveille will be ¼ hour before first light. At first light, each sub-unit will move out of the leaguer without further orders and take up its position in air formation. The Regimental Group will move into leaguer at last light, sub-units moving in on their own and taking station on RHQ. 'A' Echelon will move in facing the rear. When sub-units move out of leaguer, vehicles must be out of the leaguer before they start turning. The turning of tanks within the leaguer must be avoided.

(iv) Replenishment will be carried out immediately the leaguer is formed and the hot meal served out. Empty containers will be collected in the morning to prevent unnecessary movement within the leaguer.

(v) All returns will be rendered to the Adjutant within 30 mins. of entering the leaguer. In many cases these returns can be compiled before the leaguer is formed.

(vi) Sub-unit runners will report with their bedding to the C.Os tank as soon as the leaguer is formed.

(vii) Os.C sub-units need not report until called for. This will be when orders have been prepared for future movements and operations. If no orders are received, sub-units will move out as in (iii).

(viii) The R.S.O. will ensure that all call-signs, frequencies and codes are issued. He will also see that set maintenance and battery-changing and charging are carried out.

(ix) When the leaguer is formed, the following spare operators will be sent to the rear link tank:—1 from each Squadron and 3 from 'A' Echelon.

(x) The R.T.A. will report full details of the mechanical state of the Regiment.

(xi) It is the duty of all ranks to ensure that the leaguer is formed quickly, correctly and silently, and that all replenishment, maintenance etc. is carried out as soon as possible so that the maximum sleep may be obtained by all. During active operations quick and efficient leaguering; allowing everyone a good rest, will have a definite effect of the Regiment's future activities.

5. Recognition Signals

(a) A.F.V. Recognition Signals. Pennants will be flown on all wireless aerials as ordered by Bde H.Q.

(b) Commanders' flags will be flown until contact is gained when all distinguishing flags will be lowered.

(c) Ground to air recognition signals as ordered will be circulated by the R.S.O.

6. Codes

The current codes with extracts from the Army Map Reference Code are issued to the Regt. Code groups are issued to sub-units and changed daily.

Sub-unit commanders are issued with one copy of the above and will ensure that all tank commanders are trained in their use. The R.S.O. is responsible for distribution.

7. Camouflage

At all times, especially in leaguer, due consideration will be given to camouflage.

(a) Soil from slit trenches will be spread evenly.

(b) Nets will be used where possible.

(c) Vehicles will be parked in patches of scrub or broken ground. Make use of natural shadows.

(d) Sunshields will be worn when so ordered.

(e) Tins, blankets etc. will catch the eye of enemy aircraft and will not be left lying in the open. Blankets and clothing put out to dry must be packed away as soon as possible.

8. Reporting of Information

i. It is essential that CLEAR and CONCISE reports are always transmitted over the air, as this information must be passed back to higher formations. If reports are correctly made, the higher formation commander will be immediately in the picture. If essential information is omitted, the report is valueless.

ii. A report transmitted by a light tank commander, or by any tank commander, must contain certain types of information as under:—

(a) Time of incident.

(b) Map reference. Never refer to the enemy in terms of bearing and distance from yourself.

(c) Type and number of enemy or unknown vehicles or personnel. Much time is wasted on the air when sub-unit commanders have to ask the reporter questions.

(d) Direction of movement, whether stationary or moving, general disposition etc.

(e) Any other information.

(f) Your own actions.

iii. Example of tank commander's report:—

"At 0945 hrs., at 383407, there were 4 Mk. IV tanks and 3 M.13s stationary, facing NORTH. At 383409, there were 5 vehicles moving North-West. They look like enemy. One vehicle was pulling an anti-tank gun. They were led by a Bantam flying a red and white flag. I am moving to the high ground on my right to get better observation."

A report merely saying "I can see some tanks and transport 3000 yards to my right front" is obviously useless. The C.O. does not know where you are and must then waste time by asking a series of questions as to what type of vehicles they are and what they are doing.

iv. Reference ii.(b) above. Always find out your map reference wherever you can. If you don't know, ASK. You know the bearing of the advance and where you are in relation to the centre line, and your speedometer tells you how far you have gone. Thus you can quickly work out your own map reference at any time. Then, by knowing the bearing and distance of the enemy from your position, you can give his map reference.

v. In conclusion, a good report must contain the following information:— "WHERE IS IT, WHAT IS IT, WHAT IS IT DOING, WHAT ARE YOU DOING."

This last sentence should be written on every light tank commander's turret, so that every report should be given automatically in the correct form.

9. The Tank in Action

(a) It is the duty of the tank commander and his crew to remain in action as long as possible.

(b) The crew will never evacuate their tank unless it is on fire or has been rendered useless by enemy action.

(c) No tank will ever leave the battle line unless ordered to do so by the Squadron Commander.

(d) If a crew is forced to evacuate their tank under fire, they will not be picked up by another tank until covering fire or smoke have been put down under orders by the Squadron Commander. The same applies if a damaged tank is to be towed out of action.

Finally, it is the duty of the officers and other ranks of the Regiment to fight their tanks with the utmost vigour and offensive spirit.

10. Demolition of Tanks and 'B' Vehicles

Tanks and 'B' Vehicles which have become casualties through enemy action or owing to mechanical failure will be recovered through the usual channels.

There may be occasions when this is not possible and to avoid allowing vehicles to fall into enemy hands, the following procedure will be adopted.

'A' Vehicles.
(a) Open engine doors.
(b) Wrench rubber pipe connecting carburettor to filter.
(c) Set alight by firing Verey Pistol into running petrol. DO NOT stand close and throw lighted match as the force of explosion with the type of petrol used will be considerable.

'B' Vehicles.
With the pointed end of a pick pierce the bottom of one or two petrol tanks. Into the pool of petrol formed throw a lighted match or piece of flaming waste. With the low grade petrol used in 'B' Vehicles there is little danger of violent explosion.

If the above procedures cannot be carried out vehicles can be destroyed by fire from one's own guns.

11. Security

Security is of the utmost importance.
The following points must be carefully borne in mind and taught to all ranks.

(i) Never discuss military matters with anyone not personally known to you.
(ii) Always ask a stranger to identify himself, however senior he may be.
(iii) Do not listen to rumours, and never repeat any item of news unless you are sure it is true. This applies especially when talking to people who have just come out of action. They usually mention their own casualties before anything else and this generally grows into a lurid story which if repeated is likely to cause alarm and despondency among the more impressionable of your men.
(iv) Never speculate about troop movements or possible events because that is how unnecessary and alarmist rumours begin.
(v) Nothing must be said over the W/T which may be of use to the enemy. The use of veiled speech is secure if correctly done. It is not usually necessary to disguise the term fitter or towrope, because the enemy are

not in a position to benefit by the fact that you yourself have said over the air that you have broken down. An intelligent use of veiled speech, coupled with codewords or numerals for items of replenishment will make any R/T conversation secure.

(vi) Always use the codes as laid down in para G whenever possible. Always give the position of our own troops in code and of enemy in clear. Never correct yourself by using code in the event of you giving your position in clear by mistake.

(vii) If you are so unfortunate as to be taken prisoner, never give any other information except your NAME, RANK and NUMBER. Any other information will be of use to the enemy, and a danger to your comrades.

12. Gunnery

The art of gunnery is sometimes forgotten during the efforts of tank crews to get their tanks mechanically fit. But it must be remembered that the whole reason for having a tank is so that a gun may be taken into action against the enemy, protected by armour and over ground that would be impossible for wheels. A tank, however perfect it may be mechanically, is useless to us unless it contains a gun with which the crew can hit the enemy at effective range, and a crew that can do it.

Therefore, the importance of gunnery cannot be too greatly stressed. All members of crews must be gunnery-minded in the same way that they are maintenance minded. Continuous training must be carried out during normal training periods and even in areas of active operations, so that tank commanders and gunners will know their weapons perfectly and will react instinctively to any situation.

The following must be practiced:—

(i) Judging distance. Much ammunition is wasted on ranging shots. Judge the distance correctly, followed by bold bracketting and accuracy increases enormously. Also remember that when using solid shot, a miss is as good as a mile. Every round must hit.

(ii) Gun drill.

(iii) Points before, during and after firing.

(iv) Checking and care of ammunition and gun spares.

(v) Fire orders. A quick, accurate fire order will get your gun on to the target quickly and accurately, and it may mean the difference between the destruction of your tank and the enemy's.

(vi) Recognition of targets. Tank commanders and gunner must be able to determine immediately the type of gun (it may be a friend) or the type of vehicle or gun that has been sighted.

In conclusion, the importance of accurate gunnery must be impressed on all ranks. Good gunnery combined with good maintenance will win a tank battle. Good maintenance by itself never will.

13. Navigation

Navigation is a term used in the army to mean the art of getting accurately from place to place and of always knowing where you are. It may be the lot of a man of any rank to have to navigate himself, and it is therefore necessary that all ranks have a thorough grounding in the general principles of Navigation.

This paragraph applies more especially to light tank commanders who must know their position at all times.

The following points must therefore be borne in mind:—

1. Have the proper equipment:— Prismatic compass, sun compass if possible, map protractor, pencil, notebook, watch.

2. Know the exact map reference of your start point. If you don't know, ask.

3. Always keep an eye on your speedometer. At the end of a long run you may have to deduct up to 10% to allow for deviations off your line.

4. Continually check your position with recognisable features on the ground such as cairns, trig. points, wadis, etc.

5. Always have confidence in your own ability as a navigator and don't let others make you change your mind unless they can definitely prove you wrong. If you are wrong, admit it.

Sub-unit commanders must ensure that all ranks have practice in navigation and map reading, including night marching.

14. Miscellaneous Hints

1. Always have your essential equipment to hand and ready for use. Have your binoculars adjusted; your watch corrected to the last time signal you heard; your pencil sharpened; your compass, protractor, map case, code list, and sub-machine gun accessible.

2. Don't waste water by using too much when making tea. You can shave in an egg cup. Conserve water and food.

3. Don't throw away cigarette tins, string or old clothes. They all come in handy.

4. Don't stow so much kit on the outside of the tank that you cannot traverse your turret. Have all kit in its correct place.

5. When enemy aircraft are active, remember the following:—
    (i) Dive-bombers nearly always attack from the direction of the sun.
    (ii) They are often followed by low flying fighters from a different direction.
    (iii) Keep looking in all directions.
    (iv) Get into your tank when being attacked from the air.
    (v) Engage enemy aircraft vigorously with fire but don't waste ammunition on aircraft that are obviously out of range. Don't be a danger to your own side by using low angle fire.

6. R/T messages must be acknowledged immediately, either by the tank commander or the operator. Good wireless discipline saves much time and trouble.

7. Avoid running over tins and pieces of metal in the desert for the following reasons:—
    Material run over by a tank or vehicle is useless for salvage.
    Suspensions may get entangled and therefore damaged.
    The tin or metal may hide or even be a mine or booby trap.

8. Always try and take up a hull down position with the tank sideways or oblique to the enemy. This enables you to alter your position when you are being registered by an enemy gun.

9. Do not attend a conference without your map and notebook.

10. Always have your map or maps folded in your map case so that they will cover the day's operations.

The art of camouflage was important for all troops, to hide their presence, route, or intentions to enemy observers on the ground and in the air. Concealing the presence of a 60- or even 30-ton tank which left deep tracks on all but the hardest ground was a considerable task, and detailed manuals were issued explaining how to disguise the shape and colour of a tank with nets and paint, use shade and buildings, position tanks in leaguer to blend in with the natural patterns of the landscape, and erase signs of tracks. Different theatres required different techniques, and the Russians needed to be able to disguise their tanks in the cold and all types of snow and thaw. This article, by a colonel in the Soviet army, shows that tank commanders would need to completely alter their tactics and movements in order to remain invisible in a winter landscape.

Russian Tank Camouflage in Winter

a. General

Winter camouflage of tanks presents a problem with certain special features, created on the one hand by the general winter background, and on the other by weather conditions which greatly affect the tanks themselves and their employment under combat conditions. In winter the change in the operational characteristics of the tanks and in the conditions of employing them in combat will influence the work to be done in camouflaging them.

Winter conditions (as has been shown by combat experience) create considerable difficulties for the camouflage of tank units. In winter the principal characteristics of a region are its uniform white background, a lack of outline, and an almost complete absence of color. The only exceptions are small settlements, woods, and thick underbrush. Forests whose dense foliage provides perfect concealment in the summertime lose their masking qualities completely in the winter. In winter, on an even, white blanket of snow, camouflage is very difficult. Almost all methods of camouflage employed in summer prove inapplicable. It is necessary to make wide use of special winter covering for the vehicles, and to paint them with winter paint: all one color (protective coat) or in large spots (disruptive).

In winter, tracks made by moving vehicles can be easily recognized, not only from the air but also from high ground observation posts. The removal of tracks left by tanks is the personal responsibility of the commander of the tank units and of the crews. The presence of a blanket of snow, which is often very thick, greatly reduces the mobility of tanks, and as a result reduces the possibility of tanks appearing quickly and suddenly from directions unexpected by the enemy. Tanks cannot go through more than 3 inches of snow without appreciable loss of speed. The deepest snow through which a tank can go is 3 feet; for practical purposes tanks can operate in 1½ feet of snow. It is apparent that these conditions greatly reduce the possibility of using approach routes concealed from enemy observation. Snow makes it necessary for tanks to employ existing roads, which means that they must engage in all their combat operations in those parts of the terrain which are under the special observation of the enemy.

An important winter factor from the point of view of concealment is the longer period of darkness, which helps conceal the movement and disposition of tanks, provided, of course, that all camouflage measures are carefully observed.

Another winter factor which may be considered important from the point of view of camouflage and concealment is the greater cloudiness of the sky, which hinders reconnaissance activity by enemy aviation and sometimes stops it completely. Then too, tanks may make use of snowstorms which produce conditions of bad visibility and audibility, and as a result tend to lessen vigilance on the part of enemy observation posts.

b. Tank Painting

In winter, tanks are painted all white when the aim is to avoid observation, and in two colors with large spots when the aim is to avoid identification.

As a rule, all-white paint is employed in level, open country characterized by a lack of variegated color. Two-color disruptive winter paint is used where the ground presents a variety of color, where there are forests, underbrush, small settlements, thawed patches of earth, etc.

One-color camouflage is applied to all parts of the tank in one or two coats. For the paint, zinc white or titanium white is used only with an oil base, and slight amounts of ultramarine coloring. For the lack of anything better, the tanks may be painted with chalk dissolved in water.

Painting in two colors with large spots can be undertaken in two ways: one is to paint only part of the tank surface, leaving about ¼ or ⅓ of the tank's surface in the original green; another is to repaint the tank entirely in two colours, either white and dark gray, or white and gray-brown.

When the weather is cold, painting should take place in a warm place, since paint applied when the temperature is 10° below zero Fahrenheit is too hard to be applied.

In winter, as in summer, it is necessary to avoid mechanical repetition of patterns and colours. For example, in painting the tanks of a platoon, one or two tanks are painted white, a third in white irregular stripes leaving part of the protective green paint as it is, the fourth with white and dark gray spots, and finally, the fifth with white and grayish-brown spots.

c. Covers and Ground Masks

For winter tank camouflage, one may use nets made of cord which have fastened to them irregular white patches of fabric, about 1 yard across. A large all-white cover also may be used.

When using white winter covers, it is necessary to pay attention to the degree of whiteness of the materials used, for even if a little yellow shows or if part of the material is soiled, it will sharply outline the cover and the tank against the background of pure white snow. A simple method to improve this camouflage is to place a thin layer of snow on the cover.

In winter, ground masks are also used. But the construction of these camouflage masks involves special considerations dependent on the character of the background. The principal camouflage materials employed are irregularly shaped pieces of white fabric or painted white matting. In addition to the white patches, dark patches should be fastened to the material to give the appearance of bushes, tree tops, or other natural ground features. For dark patches one may use tree branches or other similar materials. As with covers, the use of white patches alone, or of a combination of white and dark patches, will depend entirely on the terrain and the coloration of the surroundings.

To attach the patches to the mask, they are frozen on after wetting the material with water.

d. Dummy Tanks

Drawing the attention of the enemy to enemy tanks has the same aim in wintertime as in summer, namely to deceive the enemy concerning the disposition, types, and character of tank activity. However, in winter the making of dummy tanks is subject to certain special conditions. Large dummy snow tanks may be made by packing snow into the form of a tank, showing the hull, the suspension system, and the turret, and then spraying with paint. Movable life-size models are constructed not on wheels but on skis. "Flat" models made be made simply by treading the snow into the contours of a tank. In all other respects the making and use of dummy tanks in winter is no different than in summer.

e. Camouflage while in Motion

Generally speaking, winter conditions make it necessary to move along existing roads. Since winter roads appear to the aerial observer as dark strips, tanks which have an all-white winter paint stand out fairly clearly. In view of the fact that vehicles can be spotted by the shadow they cast, they should move on the side of the road nearest the sun so that their shadow falls on the road, which is darker than the snow next to the road. Movement along the roads, especially at great speeds and over fluffy dry snow, gives itself away by clouds of snow dust. For this reason, movement of vehicles in wintertime should be at low speeds, especially over new-fallen snow. The tracks left by the tank treads stand out clearly as two dark parallel strips with tread impressions. These can be obliterated by sweeping the road. When tracks are left on the hard crust of the existing road it is necessary, instead of sweeping, to remove them with the aid of graders.

When the tanks pass through places where turns are unavoidable, there appear everywhere little heaps of upturned snow; these are characteristic marks and betray the movement of tanks. To prevent this, turns must be made gradually in a wide arc whenever practicable, or else the heaps of snow which are formed must be cleared away.

The reflection from the lenses of the tank headlights will also give away their movement. In order to prevent this, it is necessary to cover the headlights with white fabric covers, or some other material.

Finally, among the most important factors betraying the movement of tanks to ground observers is the clank of the tracks. The noise of these can be heard better as the temperature falls. Naturally, when operations are in the immediate vicinity of the enemy, one makes use not only of all the ordinary precautions employed in summer for the prevention of noise, but takes into account the special characteristics of winter weather with its increased transmission of sound.

f. Camouflage of Stationary Tanks

In winter, tanks are, generally speaking, parked alongside buildings and in woods and shrubbery; in exceptional cases it may be necessary to station tanks in open flat country or in gullies.

The peculiar characteristic of inhabited areas in wintertime from the point of view of camouflage is the motley appearance of the landscape due to the presence of dwelling places, barns, gardens, roads, and paths. This wealth and variety of outline affords considerable opportunities for concealing the position of tanks from air and ground observation by the enemy.

As a rule, all vehicles in bivouac should be placed under the roofs of sheds and barns. Only where there is insufficient number of such structures, or where the size of the vehicles makes it impossible to place the vehicles in the existing shelters, is it necessary to build shelters, resembling the existing structures in the given locality. Just as in summertime, these camouflage structures may be built either as additions to existing structures or as separate structures. The separate camouflage structures should be situated along laid-out paths, and the tracks of the caterpillars which lead to the place where the tanks are stationed should be swept or dragged so as to resemble an ordinary road.

Where there is not enough time to construct structures, it is sometimes possible (as on the outskirts of a village) to camouflage tanks by simulating haystacks, piles of brushwood, stacks of building materials, etc. This is done by strewing over the vehicle a certain quantity of material at hand and covering it with a thin layer of snow.

Woods, orchards, and brushwood can be used for camouflage purposes in the wintertime only if additional camouflage precautions are taken. Since leafy woods offer much less concealment in winter than in summer and do not hide the vehicles from air observation, they must be covered with white covers, and there should be strewn over them broken branches or some other camouflage material such as hay, straw, etc.

When there are no white covers, the vehicles may be covered with dark ones, but snow must be placed on top and scattered. Dark covers may be used only against a background which has natural black spots. Finally, if no covers of any kind are available, the vehicles should be covered with branches, straw, hay, and the like, and snow placed on top in irregular patches.

When the tanks are stationed in open flat country, then the camouflage of the tanks also involves the breaking up of the uniform aspect of the locality, which is done by treading around on the snow. Then these areas are given irregular form by scattering here and there patches of pine needles, straw, and rubbish. The ground should also be laid bare, as tanks which are painted a dark colour will not be easily discovered against a dark background, either by visual air observation or by the study of aerial photographs.

In open country, thaws are particularly favourable to the camouflage of tanks, for the disappearing snow exposes portions of the surface of the ground.

The result is that the ground assumes a naturally mottled appearance, and the contours of vehicles stationed there are easily blended.

When there is deep snow, tanks may be placed in snow niches built near snowdrifts along the road. The entrances to these should be directly off the road in order to avoid tell-tale tracks of the treads. On the top the niches are covered with white covers, or with some other available material over which snow is placed. In order to camouflage the entrance, it is necessary to use hangings of white cloth or painted mats which may be readily let down or pulled up.

When the tank is stationed in a gully, it is covered with solid white covers of any kind of fabric or matting painted white, or by the regulation nets, with white and black patches attached to it.

While the Russians had, perhaps naturally, developed detailed doctrine for operating their tanks in winter conditions, other armies realised they needed to learn how to adapt, as illustrated by the US interest in Finnish snow tank traps. This detailed explanation was published in the *American Tactical and Technical Trends* in March 1943.

FINNISH TANK TRAPS OVER FROZEN RIVERS

A recent report on the method used by the Finns to open tank-trap channels in the ice over streams and lakes, and to keep them open and hidden, may be useful for purposes of winter operations. Briefly, the Finns saw out a channel in the ice, roof it over, leaving a space underneath to prevent re-freezing, and replace the snow over the roof to keep the space and to hide the trap.

The work is not difficult. After the outline of the trap has been traced, the snow over the ice to be cut is scraped back into windrows (as in fig. 1, stage 1). Then, a channel 13 feet wide is sawn out, with the cut on the downstream side sloping outward and downward from the center, so that the ice cakes can be pushed down into the current and the channel is left clear (stage 2). Over the cut is then laid a light framework roof with either a curved, or cigar-shaped cross section of the king-post type (stage 3), made of light material. The arch provides the air space over the water. Then the snow is shovelled back (stage 4).

The best time of year for trap making is early winter, while the ice is still thin, although there must be snow enough for insulation and concealment.

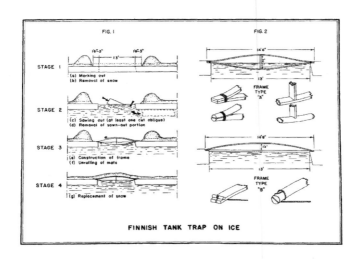

FINNISH TANK TRAP ON ICE

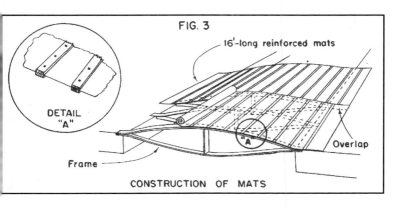

CONSTRUCTION OF MATS

117

CHAPTER 4: KNOWING THE ENEMY

Throughout the war there was intense interest in the capabilities of the enemy. Tank commanders needed to know what they were up against, a need catered for by the plethora of regularly issued official bulletins, which contained detailed reports on new enemy (and allied) AFVs, improved weapons or armour, and reports of how the enemy had used them in action. The information for these reports came from official observers, the interrogation of prisoners of war, captured documents, or the examination of captured tanks. The official journals and intelligence bulletins would be distributed to various levels, and the lessons they contained would be incorporated into training and doctrine.

Operation *Barbarossa* began on 22 June 1941, with a huge German advance into Russia across a 1,800-mile front. Around 3,570 panzers rolled into the Soviet Union, in four panzergruppen. There they found a nasty surprise, the T-34 tank. An article in *Das Reich* in June 1943 stated that, 'The T-34 used by the Russians at the opening of hostilities in 1941 was at that time the best tank produced anywhere – with its 76-mm long-barrelled gun, its tightfitting tortoise-shaped cap, the slanting sides of it's "tub", the broad cat's paw tread of its forged caterpillar chains capable of carrying this 26-ton tank across swamps and morasses no less than through the grinding sands of the steppes. ... The Soviet Union was the only nation in the world to possess, even prior to the approach of the present war, completely perfected and tried-out series of tanks.' Unsurprisingly, the Germans were very interested in examining captured T-34s, and their conclusions would influence the design of the Panzer V Panther.

By the end of 1941, the Russians had halted the German advance and German casualties totalled over 830,000. In January 1942 the exhausted German army was pushed away from Moscow. All plans for a quick defeat of the Soviet Union had to be revised: fighting on the Eastern Front would continue until the Red Army advanced into Berlin in May 1945. The failure of *Barbarossa* is the context for this paper, delivered at Panzertruppenschule II, a major panzer training school in Wünsdorf, in March 1942. The lecturer is interested in the development of Russian tanks and tactics, in order to prepare for what might come as the campaign resumes.

Russian AFVs – Technical and Tactical

We stand at the end of a hard winter of war. After the muddy spring, we will start a new offensive. The question of battle in tanks and against tanks will then be decided.

In the war with RUSSIA two highly armed nations came against each other, nations whose soldiers – albeit springing from widely different spiritual backgrounds – were equally brave fighters. Both nations possessed strong tank forces, both had good engineers and effective industries.

The 1941 campaign ended with a clear victory "on points" for the German tank arm but a "knock-out" was NOT achieved. The interval we are now entering holds for both sides the same advantages and disadvantages.

We have got to know our opponent, and must employ the pause to learn thoroughly the nature of the warfare he wages, his strong points and his weaknesses, both technically and tactically. To assist this process is the aim of this discussion.

In April of last year when, for the first time, a similar study was prepared, the only material available was HEIGL's handbook of tanks, a mass of agents' reports, and – by far the best source – accounts of the Russo-Finnish War. These provided the following picture of Russian tank development.

As early as 1923 RUSSIA procured foreign licences and began at once to build on a large scale. The T 26 goes back to VICKERS ARMSTRONG (ENGLAND). The BT is an imitation of the American Christie tank. The heavy tanks (T 28 and T 35) have strong German (BMW) influence. In this manner Russian tank strength grew very rapidly so far as numbers were concerned; they had to submit to the disadvantage of having large quantities of material which grew more seriously out of date every year.

The Russo-Finnish war, however, which gave us so many valuable pieces of information (often NOT used), conferred a great advantage on RUSSIA too. This was the opportunity of testing her armoured forces in actual warfare against an opponent utterly inferior in numbers.

Although FINLAND's peculiar geographical conditions reduce the value of these experiences as regards general principles (strategy), nevertheless the experience gained in the technical and tactical field remained of extremely high value. The result was negative.

Technically the vehicles were NOT able to fulfil what was required of them. The narrow tracks sank too deep into the ground; there was too little clearance for snow-covered surfaces; the reserve of power in the engines was too small and the armour inadequate.

Only one point was found to have been right: that of giving all tanks without exception an anti-tank weapon – i.e. a gun. With the exception of the amphibious tank all Russian AFVs, including armd cars used in the Finnish war already had 3.7ca. guns, and in some cases already 4.5 cm and 7.62 cm. Many units had failed to profit by these lessons at the time of the Russian War, and had to pay for them again in blood.

Russian manuals give much space to tank and anti-tank fighting, and offer very exact instructions. They demand tactics which to us appear above the reach of the troops and over complicated.

The Red Army's tanks were to be NOT only as a supporting arm for the inf (I tank) but also in independent units in the manner of the German Panzer Divs. Experience in FINLAND confirms that this was the intention. So-called mechanised formations (tanks, Inf. and Mot Arty) were employed in independent roles. According to their instructions they had to operate against the enemy's flank and rear, and in FINLAND this actually happened for example North of LAKE LADOGA. Inadequate recce, inexperienced leadership, and climatic hindrances were much in their way, and they failed to make an impression on the FINNS who, despite their great inferiority in numbers, fought with tenacity and skill. The Russian armd formations soon found themselves in supply difficulties, and were cut off and destroyed.

According to the manuals most of the Red Army's armd units are components of infantry divs and inf corps, i.e. a pure inf support weapon. The Russian theory divides the enemy's defensive position into three zones:—

1. That of Inf weapons using observed fire,
2. That of Inf weapons using indirect fire,
3. That of the arty.

To this sub-division corresponds the method of tank attack, which distinguishes between "Inf support" and "distant action". The RUSSIANS are inclined though to put their arty and tanks under command of even small units of infantry; in fact, Arty batteries even lose their identity and, for example, when supporting II/IR 23 become "close support Arty II/23". Similarly the RUSSIANS divide their tank forces for the attack into those for close support and those for distant action. Those for distant action are tanks armed with heavy guns and capable of a good speed (BT types) and have the role of making deep thrusts to destroy the enemy's HQ's and Arty. They have to co-operate closely with the Air Force and long range Arty. Their attack is usually a prelude to the main attack, but the manuals provide for their use in following up. Every div in the attack should receive at least a Bn of tanks for distant action. These have to break through in a dense mass on a front of 300–1000 metres, with arty protection in front and on the flanks.

Close support tanks have heavier armour but are slower. Their function is direct support of the Inf from which they must never become separated by more than 500–600 metres. These close support tanks have to co-operate closely with the Fd. Arty. They are frequently sub-allotted right down to Inf Pls, and as a general rule one Sqn of tanks is used in support of each forward Inf Bn. If the enemy is regarded as strong, the close support tanks can be divided into two waves, one to give immediate support and the other for more independent action.

In the Finnish War the RUSSIANS appear to have attacked in this complicated manner on the Karelian Isthmus. The result was that formations fell into total confusion, and the attack was held up with heavy losses. It was found that the tactical principles taught in the manuals were out of all relation to the technical qualities of the weapons and the capabilities of officers and men.

Admittedly, the FINNS reported a tank type with 60 mm armour weighing over 40 tons (the T 35c). They described the morale of the tank crews as good; crews of tanks knocked out would refuse to surrender and rather perish. Tanks immobilised went on firing with all their weapons. The officers were described as fanatical and tenacious.

What have we learned from this campaign? Little, it must honestly be admitted. We underestimated Russian morale, Russian power of organisation and Russian adaptability. Then came June 22nd. The Campaign in the East began.

As expected, masses of enemy tanks appeared in action, usually with insufficient armour and badly led, but always mounting guns and fighting with invariable courage. Soon, however, we met with new tank types. And our rounds glanced harmlessly off armour of unsuspected strength. The Russian tanks were now mounting guns of 7.62 cm, even of 15.20 cm. The surprise was an unpleasant one; we must NOT lay ourselves open to it again.

The Russians had learned their lesson in the Finnish War, and learned it thoroughly. They obviously set to work at once with all their energy and we must admit that they made a good job. Fortunately HITLER's bold decision did NOT allow them sufficient time. New types had to be used during "teething troubles" with crews still insufficiently trained. Even so, they gave us a lot of trouble. The RUSSIAN will NOT leave unused the breathing space he now has. Let us NOT again underestimate him. Though a great part of his industrial plant has been destroyed or occupied, the initial capacity of Russian industry was enormous and it is still very considerable. In the Spring of 1942 the SOVIET UNION will again put in the field an armoured force numerically much superior to ours; the decisive battle between our tanks and theirs, our anti-tank guns and theirs, has still to come.

In the whole of the Eastern campaign the RUSSIANS appear never to have attacked along the lines laid down in their manuals. We need NOT count on their doing so in the future.

Everywhere Russian tanks attacked in close co-operation with infantry and more probably under control of the infantry. Comparatively small groups of tanks (5–10 vehicles) were followed by small bodies of infantry, or the inf sat on the tanks, or was drawn on skis by the tanks.

Russian tactics therefore never made use of the mass attack but could, on the other hand, use tanks at innumerable points.

We must get rid of the idea that tanks will only appear where they can attack on a regimental front. These very small bodies of tanks can attack even in unfavourable tank country (thin woods, village streets, etc). In face of a tank attack in such small numbers a tank barrier, placed even only a few hundred yards behind the advanced position, is valueless, since the tanks have in any case only very limited objectives.

The German anti-tank gunner must realise clearly that he will be attacked, NOT according to German tank tactics, but according to Russian.

Small groups of tanks consist usually of 3–5 tanks of various types. The practice of combining light and heavy tanks seems to have developed into a principle.

The attack was slow in developing, almost hesitant. Russian tanks frequently opened fire at great ranges (2000 metres and over) at recognised or only suspected targets.

In tank v tank battles, the RUSSIANS tried to make the contest a long range one.

These tactics show proper appreciation of their superiority in armament. The German tank must endeavour to exploit its mechanical superiority and better visibility in order to conduct the battle at ranges decided by itself.

Russian tanks advance slowly from sector to sector, giving mutual fire support. This was the case when only two tanks operated. As the visibility from Russian tanks is so bad, the Russians usually observed with glasses from the open turret (Pick off!). The turret door was frequently open (Thrust boughs in, hand-grenades).

When the front was penetrated the heaviest tank (frequently the Kw) halted to observe, while light tanks advanced on the right and left. Anti-tank guns were thereby compelled to open fire. But if they were identified by the heavy tanks – which was by NO means always the case – the heavily armoured tank then usually attacked immediately and while on the move, NOT, however, employing its guns to any great extent, but overrunning the A.Tk gun (Mines in front of A.Tk guns!)

In other cases the heavy tank first penetrated the position, halted there and attempted to neutralise the A.Tk guns while light tanks attacked. When anti-tank guns were identified they were overrun. (Single halted tanks to be attacked immediately with close-combat weapons!)

Frequently heavy tanks halted on reaching their limited objectives or returned to their starting line. (All-round observation!)

According to many reports, tanks appeared to drive blindly across country. This can probably be attributed to chance destruction of the driver's vision slits by MG fire (such destruction must become the rule!).

The RUSSIANS also used small groups of tanks in night attacks in conjunction with powerful and concentrated searchlights. Experience in the EAST and experiment on the range have shown that searchlights are very difficult to hit (single shots from a telescopic sighted rifle are most likely to succeed). We must expect such night attacks on a larger scale in future. The searchlight was always fixed to a very heavily armoured tank and naturally attracted fire. Light tanks advancing on the flanks thereupon engaged anti-tank guns disclosed by flashes.

If the Russian tanks succeeded in catching an anti-tank gun or similar target in the beam, it thereupon took a line upon the gun, switched off the S/L and drove blind at the gun in order to crush it.

The principle of attacking with small bodies of tanks can only be met effectively by the proper co-ordination of all defensive weapons.

Tanks. Knowledge of Russian tanks is a matter of life and death for the German tank soldier. The armour ("can I penetrate?") and the armament ("will my own armour be penetrated at this distance?") must be known.

A German tank which, for example, meets an opponent with superior armour must direct his fire at the tracks and endeavour to delay the enemy attack in order to give the heavier weapons (7.5 cm tank gun with hollow charge or 8.8 cm Flak) the necessary time to come into action.

According to agents' reports the RUSSIANS are now forming tank bns composed of one heavy Coy (KV?) one medium Coy (T 34?) and two light Coys (thirty T 60 and five T 34). Whether they are in a position to carry this out on a large scale we do NOT know. In itself this organisation seems a probable one since it represents a logical application of the methods of attack which they have been using in the Eastern front. The Russian tank arm was revealed here in all its strength, but also in its weakness.

This treatise is intended for officers and NOT for the press. Any tendencious optimism has therefore been intentionally avoided. Every soldier, from time immemorial, has considered his opponents' weapons better than his own. Even on the range, it is always the rifle that's wrong when he misses. And in support of his pseudo heroism he must always report that "the enemy fights excellently with superb weapons". An officer should never be guilty of this attitude and should also discourage it in his men, for any kind of exaggeration, NO matter how harmless it may seem, is dangerous.

It is, however, astonishing that so many troops who have been in battle with Russian tanks should always have had 52 or even 64, 80 or 120 ton tanks against them. Loose talking detracts from morale.

It was commonly said that Russian tanks were completely impervious to 3.7 cm and even 5 cm anti-tank guns. That is NOT true, nor will it become true.

Neither the old tanks nor the new mass-produced T 60 are impervious. The T 34 and KW are almost so, which is quite sufficient. Officers must have an exact knowledge of enemy tanks in order to estimate their dangerousness. Careless and false reports can only be corrected by one who knows his enemy thoroughly.

The great numbers of the Russian tanks are NOT a deciding factor. 1941 has proved that.

Nor is thickness of armour; for we have NOT been asleep, but have discovered counter-measures.

<u>In Tactics</u> – from the Commander of the tanks down to the driver – we have complete superiority.

1942 will show as before:

<u>It is NOT the machine that decides, but the man behind it.</u>

In the mid-1930s, the Red Army had had the largest number of armoured vehicles and tank units in the world, but Stalin's purges hit the army's officer corps hard, destroying the collective knowledge of the army, and drastically slowing tank production. Training also dropped to very low levels. However, as the Germans realised, on the eve of war the Soviet Union had some of the best tanks in the world. Moreover, the Red Army could field around 23,000 tanks; this number did include a lot of older tanks, many tanks were poorly maintained, and there were shortages of ammunition and radios.

Poor radio communications limited the tactics that Soviet tanks could employ against the Germans. They could follow their platoon leader, or proceed towards a pre-arranged destination, but complex manoeuvres were unworkable. The advantage they did have over the Germans was knowledge of the terrain, and numbers, which they combined with speed. The battle of Kursk, in the summer of 1943, was one of the largest tank battles in history. The Germans had committed around 3,000 tanks to the operation, *Citadel*, which the Soviets countered with over 5,000 tanks.

These Russian tactics, with details of the weak points on specific German tanks, were translated for *Tactical and Technical Trends* 16 (January 1943), but were probably written before the Tiger I saw action on the Eastern Front.

Russian tank tactics against German tanks

a. Manner of conducting fire for the destruction of enemy tanks

For the successful conduct of fire against enemy tanks, we should proceed as follows:

(1) While conducting fire against enemy tanks, and while maneuvering on the battlefield, our tanks should seek cover in partially defiladed positions.

(2) In order to decrease the angle of impact of enemy shells, thereby decreasing their power of penetration, we should try to place our tanks at an angle to the enemy.

(3) In conducting fire against German tanks, we should carefully observe the results of hits, and continue to fire until we see definite signs of a

hit (burning tanks, crew leaving the tank, shattering of the tank or the turret). Watch constantly enemy tanks which do not show these signs, even though they show no signs of life. While firing at the active tanks of the enemy, one should be in readiness to renew that battle against those apparently knocked out.

b. Basic types of German tanks and their most vulnerable parts

The types of tanks most extensively used in the German Army are the following: the 11-ton Czech tank, the Mark III, and the Mark IV. The German self-propelled assault gun (Sturmgeschütz) has also been extensively used.

In addition to the above-mentioned types of tanks, the German Army uses tanks of all the occupied countries; in their general tactical and technical characteristics, the armament and armor, these tanks are inferior.

(1) Against the 11-ton Czech tank, fire as follows:
> (a) From the front—against the turret and gun-shield, and below the turret gear case;
> (b) From the side—at the third and fourth bogies, against the driving sprocket, and at the gear case under the turret;
> (c) From behind—against the circular opening and against the exhaust vent.

Remarks: In frontal fire, with armor-piercing shells, the armor of the turret may be destroyed more quickly than the front part of the hull. In firing at the side and rear, the plates of the hull are penetrated more readily than the plates of the turret.

(2) Against Mark III tanks, fire as follows:
> (a) From the front—at the gun mantlet and at the driver's port, and the machine-gun mounting;
> (b) From the side—against the armor protecting the engine, and against the turret ports;
> (c) From behind—directly beneath the turret, and at the exhaust vent.

Remark: In firing from the front against the Mark III tank, the turret is more vulnerable than the front of the hull and the turret gear box. In firing from behind, the turret is also more vulnerable than the rear of the hull.

(3) Against the self-propelled assault gun, fire as follows:

(a) From the front—against the front of the hull, the driver's port, and below the tube of the gun;

(b) From the side—against the armor protecting the engine, and the turret.

(c) From behind—against the exhaust vent and directly beneath the turret.

(4) Against the Mark IV, fire as follows:

(a) From the front—against the turret, under the tube of the gun, against the driver's port, and the machine-gun mounting;

(b) From the side—at the center of the hull, at the engine compartment, and against the turret port.

(c) From behind—against the turret, and against the exhaust vent.

Remarks: It should be noted that in firing against the front of this tank, the armor of the turret is more vulnerable than the front plate of the turret gear box, and of the hull. In firing at the sides of the tank, the armour plate of the engine compartment and of the turret, is more vulnerable than the armor plate of the turret gear box.

In 1941 Hitler wanted a well-armoured heavy tank that could out-gun all enemy tanks. The development of a suitable tank was further accelerated by German experiences with the Soviet T-34 and KV tanks. Designs by Porsche and Henschel, both heavy tanks mounting the same turret featuring a massive 8.8cm gun, were presented to Hitler on his birthday, 20 April 1942. In July Henschel was contracted to mass-produce the 60-ton Panzer VI Model E 'Tiger', probably the most famous tank of the war even though only 1,349 were ever built. The first four to roll off the production line in August were rushed off to the Eastern Front.

The first Tiger tanks first saw action near Leningrad in September. The terrain restricted their use, and several Tigers broke down, but the protection that the armour afforded the crew was undeniable – 'absolute safety' must have been an unfamiliar sensation to the crews! This account was written by a German officer who, according to the note in the *Intelligence Bulletin* in which it was published, led the first Tiger I tanks into action.

Report of the First Tiger I in action

When I last saw you I promised you a brief report of our action. As I now have a few minutes to spare, I am able to keep my promise.

The action took place South of Lake Ladoga where the terrain was very unfavourable for using the "Tiger"; our advance was impeded everywhere and made impossible by swamps and morasses.

At the very beginning, during loading at Fallingbostel, we had a tank out of action owing to trouble in the transmission, but it was taken along with us. The next two instances of transmission trouble occurred on the first day in RUSSIA. The only tank left in operating condition was sent out on security patrol. There is no point in writing about the further technical difficulties and shortcomings as you are probably familiar with all of them. I shall now give you a short description of our two attacks.

The first attack was on 16 September. At 1700 hours we advanced against an invisible enemy. We faced enemy infantry and artillery. It was the first time that I fired the gun against the enemy. Here is my judgement:—

I was, and still am, enthusiastic. I was even more enthusiastic because all vehicles returned undamaged. The confidence of the men which had been somewhat shaken by the technical failures, was once again growing. Therefore, we went to the second attack unworried and with good spirits. However, here we had very bad luck. First of all, the terrain was impossible for us and in this swampy, wooded country, we sustained unfortunate hits, e.g. the guns of 3 tanks were damaged. A shell hit my own tank, struck the left side of the gun, tore the barrel, the projectile passed through the inside of the barrel and thus put the tank out of action; a second hit scored a direct hit on the driver's hatch.

By these and similar hits two tanks were severely damaged; the latter tank was burnt out and cannot be recovered. The most important thing we have noted is that no shot had penetrated the armour. One has a feeling of absolute safety when one sits inside the tank. I hope that the next attack can be carried out under different conditions.

Tiger tanks first saw action in North Africa in December 1942. With an armour-piercing round the Tiger could puncture the side or rear armour of a Sherman from over 3km away, and the thicker front armour from 1,800m. The M4 Shermans and Churchills usually couldn't get close enough to be able to penetrate its armour. On 14 February 1943, two panzer divisions, spearheaded by Tigers, inflicted heavy casualties on the inexperienced American forces at Sidi Bou Zid, destroying 100 tanks.

The Germans were not the only ones introducing new tanks into North Africa. This report from 25 Tank Brigade notes the effect of the Churchill (Infantry Mk IV) tank on the enemy: 'The Churchill surprised the Germans. As the surprise wears off, so, doubtless, will the effect to a degree. The following is an extract from an official interrogation of a prisoner of war taken during the engagements at El Aroussa on 27–28 February 1943:— "Asked to account for the fiasco of February 26 PW said 'It was the tanks. We knew of course you had some tanks here, what we did not know was that they were Churchills. That's what upset our calculations'."'

Tigers were not invulnerable, but the Allies had to adopt specific tactics in order to counter their advantages, as noted in this report following a New Zealand division's first contact with Tiger I tanks in the battle for Florence in 1944: 'A Tiger observed 5,000 yards away was engaging three Shermans. It brewed up one Sherman while the other two withdrew over a crest. A 17-pr was brought up to within 2,000 yards and engaged the Tiger side on. When the Tiger realised that it was being engaged by a H.V. gun it swung round to 90 degrees so that its heavy front armour was towards the gun. In the ensuing duel one shot hit the turret, another the suspension, while two near misses probably ricocheted into the tank. The tank was not put out of action. The range was too great to expect skill but our tactics were to make the Tiger expose its flank to the Shermans at a range of about 500 yards by swinging round to the anti-tank gun. This he did, and on being engaged by the Shermans it withdrew.'

The June 1943 article in *Das Reich* acknowledged the danger posed by the M4 Sherman: 'German soldiers have demonstrated their ability to deal with this tank; but they know the danger represented by these tanks when they appear in larger herds.' M4 Shermans had become the standard medium tank used by the British by the autumn of 1943, able to support infantry and also undertake the fast, mobile role. Following losses in the Western Desert, and examination of a captured Tiger I, it was decided that a better armed tank was needed. The A30 Challenger proved unsatisfactory and so in late 1943, work began to mount a 17-pdr in the Sherman. Following successful tests in January 1944 the tank, later dubbed the Sherman Firefly, was rushed into production. Fireflies were delivered in time for the invasion of Normandy, where they repaid the effort, perhaps most notably on 8 August when a Sherman Firefly knocked out three Tigers in 12 minutes, including that of the acclaimed tank ace SS-Hauptsturmführer Michael Wittmann, who claimed over 130 enemy tank kills and almost as many anti-tank guns. A veteran of Poland, the Balkans and *Barbarossa*, in Normandy Wittman was a company commander in Schwere SS-Panzer-Abteilung 101 (SS Heavy Panzer Battalion 101). At Villers-Bocage on 13 June, his five Tigers had destroyed around 14 Allied tanks, two anti-tank guns and 13–15 other vehicles in less than 15 minutes.

Having captured their own Tiger tank to study in early 1943, the Soviet Union developed the IS series of heavy tank, named after Joseph Stalin. The IS-I went into service in October 1943, but was soon replaced by successive up-gunned models, including the IS-2 which went into service in April 1944. This article, describing encounters between Tiger and Stalin tanks, was published in the official panzer journal, *Nachrichtenblatt der Panzertruppen*, in September 1944.

'Tiger' versus 'Stalin'

A 'Tiger' squadron reports one of a number of engagements in which it knocked out 'Stalin' tanks:

The squadron had been given the task of counter-attacking an enemy penetration into a wood, and exploiting success.

At 1215 hrs the squadron moved off together with a rifle battalion. The squadron was forced to move in file because of the thick forest, bad visibility (50 m) and narrow path. The Soviet infantry withdrew as soon as the 'Tigers' appeared. The anti-tank guns which the enemy had brought up only ¾-hour after initial penetration were quickly knocked out, partly by fire, partly by crushing.

The point troop having penetrated a further 2 km into the forest, the Troop Commander suddenly heard the sound of falling trees and observed right ahead the large muzzle-brake of the 'Stalin'. He immediately ordered: 'AP – fixed sights – fire' but was hit at the same time by two rounds from a 4.7cm anti-tank gun which obscured his vision completely. Meanwhile the second tank in the troop had come up level with the Troop Commander's tank. The latter, firing blind, was continuing the fire-fight at a range of 35m and the 'Stalin' withdrew behind a hillock. The second 'Tiger' had in the meantime taken the lead and fired three rounds at the enemy tank. It was hit by a round from the enemy's 12.2cm tank-gun on the hull below the wireless operator's seat but no penetration was effected, probably because the 'Tiger' was oblique to the enemy. The 'Stalin', however, had been hit in the gun by the 'Tiger's' last round and put out of action. A second 'Stalin' attempted to cover the first tank's withdrawal but was also hit by one of the leading 'Tigers' just below the gun and brewed up. The rate of fire of the 'Stalin' was comparatively slow.

The Squadron Commander has drawn the following conclusions from all the engagements his squadron has had with 'Stalin' tanks:

(1) Most 'Stalin' tanks will withdraw on encountering 'Tigers' without attempting to engage in a fire-fight.

(2) 'Stalin' tanks generally only open fire at ranges over 2,200 yards and then only if standing oblique to the target.

(3) Enemy crews tend to abandon tanks as soon as hit.

(4) The Russians make great efforts to prevent 'Stalin' tanks falling into our hands and particularly strive to recover or blow up such of them as have been immobilised.

(5) 'Stalin' tanks can be brewed up although penetrations are by no means easy against the frontal armour at long ranges (another 'Tiger' battalion reports that 'Stalin' tanks can only be penetrated by 'Tigers' frontally under 550 yds).

(6) 'Stalin' tanks should, wherever possible, be engaged in flanks or rear and destroyed by concentrated fire.

(7) 'Stalin' tanks should not be engaged by 'Tigers' in less than troop strength. To use single 'Tigers' is to invite their destruction.

(8) It is a useful practice to follow up the first hit with AP on the 'Stalin' tank with HE, to continue blinding the occupants.

Opinion of the Inspector-General of Panzer Troops:

(1) These experiences agree with those of other 'Tiger' units and are correct.

(2) Reference para 4, it would be desirable for the enemy to observe the same keenness in all our 'Tiger' crews. "No 'Tiger' should ever be allowed to fall into the enemy's hands intact".

(3) Reference paras 5 and 6, faced as we are now with the 12.2 cm tank-gun and 5.7cm anti-tank gun in Russia and the 9.2cm anti-aircraft/anti-tank gun in Western Europe and Italy, 'Tigers' can no longer afford to ignore the principles practised by normal tank formations.

This means, inter alia, that 'Tigers' can no longer show themselves on crests 'to have a look round' but must behave like other tanks – behaviour of this kind caused the destruction by 'Stalin' tanks of three 'Tigers' recently, all crews being killed with the exception of two men.

This battalion was surely not unacquainted with the basic principle of tank tactics that tanks should only cross crests in a body and by rapid bounds, covered by fire – or else detour around the crest. The legend of the 'thick hide', the 'invulnerability' and the 'safety' of the 'Tiger', which has sprung up in other arms of the service, as well as within the tank arm, must now be destroyed and dissipated.

Hence, instruction in the usual principles of tank versus tank action becomes of specific importance for 'Tiger' units.

(4) Reference para 7, though this train of thought is correct, 3 'Tigers' should not withdraw before 5 'Stalins' merely because the 'Tigers' do not form a proper troop. Particularly with conditions as they are at the moment, circumstances may well arise where full troops will not be readily available. And it is precisely the tank versus tank action which is decided more by superior tactics than superior numbers. However it is still true to say that single tanks invite destruction.

(5) It may be added that the 'Stalin' tank will not only be penetrated in flanks and rear by 'Tigers' and 'Panthers' but also by PzKpfw IV, and assault guns.

The Second World War was a global conflict, which meant that tank units were deployed to entirely new environments and against new enemies. The Western Desert had presented a unique set of challenges to tankers, and they had responded by adapting tactics and training; operating in the jungle and on Pacific islands required further adaptation.

Creating official manuals took time, so details of successful actions and tactics used in new environments were shared in bulletins. This report, on Australian tanks being used in fighting against the Japanese in New Guinea in November 1943, was published in the British *Notes from Theatres of War 17: Far East, April–November 1943*, with detailed 'lessons' for the use of tanks in jungle.

Tanks in New Guinea

This report is based on the report of an official observer. It does not necessarily represent the official views of the commanders in the South West Pacific Area, although it is generally in agreement with War Office doctrine.

Narrative

For the first time since the operations at MILNE BAY in August–September 1942, tanks were used by the Australian forces in the attack on SATELBERG which followed the FINSCHHAFEN landing in October 1943. In this operation MATILDA tanks were used in contrast to the STUART light tanks used at MILNE BAY.

The narrow track which runs up to SATELBERG from the coast through thick jungle is very steep, with a glassy surface in hot weather which caused the tanks some difficulty.

On 13 Nov the tanks reached their advanced camp where they carried out several days' training with the infantry battalion that they were to support, and also sand-table exercises.

The attack began on 17 Nov, with one troop of tanks in support of one company of infantry. There was stiff opposition from MGs and bunkers sited to cover the road; visibility was limited by dense bamboo. The infantry were in communication with the tanks by 'walky-talky' sets which were working well.

About 1500 hrs the leading tank had a track blown off by an unexploded 25-pr shell. This completely blocked any further progress by the tanks, since the track was too narrow for passing. Taking advantage of the situation, a small number of Japs succeeded in getting up to the second tank and throwing some unidentified explosive against the front. This had the effect of blowing the Besa back into the turret of the tank where, with the usual reliability of British weapons, it continued to fire another six rounds. Fortunately only two men suffered very minor injuries.

A perimeter was formed around the leading tank and the track was eventually repaired, the crew having been closed down for about eight hours and the tank being scarred with much small arms fire. During the day 120 rounds of 3-in How, 11,700 rounds of Besa, and 234 rounds of 2-pr HE had been expended. Considerable headway had been made, and the infantry's casualties were very light.

The following day, using a composite troop of two 2-pr tanks and one 3-in how tank further progress was made. Two 37-mm guns, a number of MGs, and possibly one heavy gun were destroyed.

Resistance stiffened the next day and the enemy positions being sited well off the road made it difficult for the tanks to approach them. At this stage the technique was for the tanks to move forward 10 to 15 yds at a time, spraying the area with Besa and HE fire. The Japs had dug anti-tank ditches and were using some mines, but these were ineffective against the tanks, although they caused the infantry some inconvenience.

One tank was temporarily disabled by a hit on a track adjuster. Altogether the tanks knocked out 12 to 15 MG positions. The 'walky-talky' was proving very successful.

Still the advance continued up the steep approaches to the mission. At one stage the tanks left the track by a road prepared by sappers and infantry, which enabled them to engage a pocket of resistance holding up the infantry on the left flank. On 25 Nov the infantry entered SATELBERG, from which the enemy had withdrawn. The final attack was assisted by a further troop of tanks which had moved up on to the high ground on the right flank. The approach to this area was the worst encountered and the tanks were preceded by a bull-dozer. Their success in negotiating the appalling country amazed everyone, including the tank crews.

A further attack using tanks and infantry was now in progress along the coast, and in spite of being slowed up by the destruction of numerous bridges, entered BONGA on the 29th.

Jap Anti-tank Weapons
The two troops of tanks that took part came out covered in bullet marks, but the Jap weapons made no impression on them at all, except for a lucky hit by a 37-mm on the suspension of one tank, necessitating minor repairs.

The mines met caused no damage whatever to the tank tracks, perhaps because of the very small size of the Jap anti-tank mine. Since this operation they have increased the effectiveness of their mines and tanks have been held up by cleverly hidden mine-fields.

British Weapons
The 3-in how has proved itself a good weapon for this type of warfare and was the chief weapon used by the squadron for bringing destructive fire on to enemy positions. Most of the fire was, however, from MGs.

Subsequent experiments have shown that 75-mm HE with delayed fuze is the most effective weapon against the bunker type of defence. It has a much greater effect than either the 3-in how or the 2-pr.

Summary
There is no doubt that the tanks played a very important part in the capture of the strong SATELBERG position. It is estimated that, apart from the MG positions destroyed, they killed at least 50 Japs and wounded a further 150.

The Australian division taking part in these operations were most impressed by the performance of the tanks, and it is generally felt that they will be invaluable for use along tracks or other suitable areas of jungle.

Lessons

(a) The secret in using tanks in jungle is detailed study of the ground. It is useless to try and use six tanks where there is only scope for three.

(b) Preliminary training with infantry must be carried out in detail.

(c) Protective infantry detachments for the tanks will always be required both during an attack and to form a defensive perimeter by night. In harbour, tanks must be closely guarded, even to the extent of digging in a MG for each tank.

(d) 'Walky-talky' sets can be used with great success for indicating targets.

(e) Drivers must learn to search the ground in front of their tanks for mines. They must learn to avoid any disturbance in the ground or anything else of a suspicious nature.

(f) When moving up a track the guns of each of the two leading tanks must be allocated a certain arc, while the third tank's gun is employed in a swinging role. The infantry follow close in behind.

(g) Maintenance must be stressed to the absolute maximum, and everything possible done while the tanks are still in the back area. Maintenance cannot be done in the dark, since every sound attracts MG fire.

An updated version of *Military Training Pamphlet 52: Warfare in the Far East* was published by the War Office in 1944, and includes a section explaining how tanks could be used in jungle country.

TANKS

Provided that the ground can be carefully reconnoitred, experience shows that tanks, driven resolutely and with skill, can frequently be used in jungle country and that their use is generally decisive. Tank personnel must be trained to reconnoitre on foot, if necessary, with infantry patrols.

Although it will generally be impossible to use tanks in large numbers, the principle of concentration should be observed when possible. Provided the tanks even in small numbers, can be brought forward, they may offer a solution to the problems of the destruction of enemy fieldworks, and the close support of infantry on to their objectives.

In jungle, tanks must at all times work in the closest co-operation with infantry, whose intimate protection they need. Without such protection they are at the mercy of enemy ambushes and of short range explosive and incendiary weapons. In country with very limited vision, tanks may have to move with turret flaps open, and the escorting infantry must deal with tree snipers.

Tanks in harbour should always be protected by infantry.

Jungle imposes a severe strain on tanks and their crews, and exceptionally long periods for rest and maintenance are essential.

The most important task of tanks in the jungle attack is to provide direct support for the assaulting infantry. They are admirably suited for destroying located enemy posts by fire from short ranges, and providing covering fire until the last few yards of the assault.

In thick jungle it may be necessary to reconnoitre for firing positions on foot and then to cut tracks through the jungle to these positions. Tank crews must be prepared to accompany infantry patrols. The thicker the jungle, the closer must be the protection of tanks by infantry. The tank inevitably draws the enemy's fire, and in light jungle, escorts must remember this danger and refrain from moving immediately alongside or behind the tanks that they are protecting.

Provided the ground is suitable, there are advantages in tanks and assaulting infantry moving on different axes.

(a) The enemy's attention is distracted, and his fire is aimed at the tank.

(b) The tank is well placed to provide flanking fire for the last few yards of the assault.

(c) Where the enemy defences are sited on the top of steep-sided hills, although the slopes may not be an insuperable bar to tank movements, an approach round the side of the feature may provide better tank going.

If tanks are employed on a different axis from the infantry, they must themselves be covered by infantry patrols on their outer flank.

In thick country there is less danger to the tank from the anti-tank gun. Tanks can normally remain longer on the objective to deal with the immediate counter-attack during consolidation, than in open country warfare, *provided that they are adequately protected from short range enemy anti-tank weapons, for example, bazookas and magnetic grenades.*

The Burma campaign of 1944 saw some of the most severe fighting in the South-East Asian theatre. In March the Japanese launched Operation *U-Go*, aiming to destroy the Allied forces at Kohima and Imphal and invade India. They cut the road between the two at the end of March 1944, encircling Imphal, and the battle raged until the Japanese finally retreated on 22 June.

Red Hill was on the Tiddim Road, between Imphal and Bishenpur, where some of the fiercest fighting of the battle took place. The Battle of Red Hill, 20–28 May 1944, was the closest the Japanese got to Imphal from the south, and the action described below took place on 28 May (though the report says April).

There was little tank against tank fighting in the Burma campaigns, as the Japanese learnt to avoid encounters with the bigger, better armed and armoured Allied tanks; the only known engagement at Imphal involved a captured M3 Stuart. However the Japanese infantry launched aggressive and tenacious attacks on tanks and their crews, meaning that infantry support for tanks was crucial. This narrative was written by an officer of the Royal Armoured Corps and published in *Current Reports from Overseas* with a comment: 'This account shows the type of action that tank commanders may be called upon to undertake in hilly jungle. The close co-operation of sapper and infantry working parties is generally necessary, and bulldozers have also often been used. Getting the tanks into positions may be slow work, but it is nearly always worth while.'

The Attack on Red Hill, 28 May 44

This narrative was written by an officer of the Royal Armoured Corps

"The Japanese had occupied in some strength three small features known as RED HILL, FIRST PIMPLE, and SECOND PIMPLE (*see* Sketch 2), just east of Milestone 10 on the IMPHAL–BISHENPUR Road, and immediately overlooking the headquarters of an Indian infantry division. The greater part of Red Hill was captured by a Baluch battalion on 25 Apr, but further attempts to advance failed.

"On 26 Apr, Major 'X' and I made a reconnaissance to determine whether tanks could get up on to RED HILL to assist the infantry. Heavy rain had fallen previous to our reconnaissance, and the ground had a thin film of mud over it. Our decision was that the climb would be an even chance if we had two days' sunshine, and the sappers put in about six hours' work in three places. The route we chose crossed the nullah and climbed on to FISH by the spur running towards the South (*see* Sketch 1). Having gained the summit of

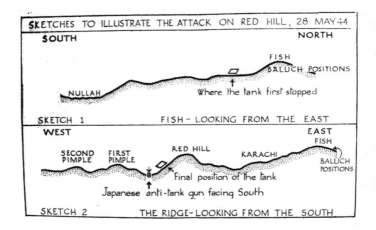

SKETCHES TO ILLUSTRATE THE ATTACK ON RED HILL, 28 MAY 44

SOUTH   NORTH

                                              FISH
                                    BALUCH POSITIONS

        NULLAH   Where the tank first stopped

SKETCH 1   FISH – LOOKING FROM THE EAST

WEST   EAST
                                                         FISH
        SECOND   FIRST   RED HILL   KARACHI
        PIMPLE   PIMPLE   BALUCH
                                                     POSITIONS
                        Final position of the tank

        Japanese anti-tank gun facing South

SKETCH 2   THE RIDGE- LOOKING FROM THE SOUTH

FISH, we were then to turn left towards the West and move along the ridge to
RED HILL (see Sketch 2).

"This reconnaissance was confirmed the next day, though it was considered
that the slit trenches on the Baluch position on FISH would prove a definite
obstacle even if they were filled in. RE work was started and in two hours there
was an even track up to the foot of FISH, where the tank is shown in Sketch 1.

"In the early morning of 28 Apr, I again went up the hill, but found that
the nullah at the bottom had almost doubled its proportions and was now
about 50 yds across and about 3ft deep.

"The surface of the spur seemed to have improved and it was not so
muddy. However, on account of the nullah, I reported to Brigadier 'Y' that I
considered it a three to one chance against a tank making the ascent.

"At about 1200 hrs I received orders to make the attempt. Grousers had
been put on every third track plate, and the tanks had the best engines in the
squadron. Coming out of harbour my own tank slipped a track and I had to
take the spare tank. We started off very determined to prove that, what we said
was impossible, could be done, and we soon reached the nullah. I was walking
in front of my tank, and I found that it was easier to guide it in this way than
from the turret. The tanks stood back in the paddy about 30 yds from the nullah and then raced at it in third gear and got successfully across, and the ascent

was begun. By 1230 hrs I was able to report my position as just South of FISH (see Sketch 1). Immediately the sappers began filling in the Baluch trenches, and I went forward to make sure of my route on to RED HILL.

"Some trenches on KARACHI and RED HILL were filled in. At 1330 hrs the first attempt to climb FISH was made, but failed owing to the loose damp earth that had been thrown out of the trenches, and to the steepness of the slope. Five or six times we tried but in vain. My tank kept slipping to the left and going dangerously near the khudside. I guided the tank backwards to its original position just South of FISH and we decided to put in another hour's sapper work and then try again. This time the sappers made a definite track, banking it up on the left hand side like a speed track. After we had had some excellent K rations, we started off again and were successful.

"My tank was halted at KARACHI and I went forward to RED HILL to receive orders from Lieutenant-Colonel 'Z' of the Gurkhas. Zero hour was fixed for 1530 hrs, and at 1535 hrs I was to cross RED HILL and fire on to FIRST PIMPLE and later on to SECOND PIMPLE (see Sketch 2). I was to cease firing HE on a red Verey light signal and was then to fire three AP shots.

"At 1530 hrs hell seemed to be let loose, and every gun, mortar and grenade known in the world appeared to be firing at the far slope of RED HILL about 20 yds from us. Our barrage had begun. I raced back to my tank, mounted, and in about three minutes we were off on to RED HILL, without mishap, where the Gurkhas were bobbing up and down throwing grenades while others worked their way round to the South flank. From the top of the hill I found that the guns could not be depressed on to either PIMPLE, so I had to advance over the hill and down the far slope.

"Three Japs ran out as I went over, but the Gurkhas were good and killed them before they reached the tank. We were able to hold the tank on the slope with the engine, both sticks pulled tight back, and the operator tugging on the parking brake with both hands. We immediately opened rapid fire on FIRST PIMPLE with 5 rounds HE from the 75 mm gun, and fired two Browning belts at about 15 Nips who ran away over the top of FIRST PIMPLE as we came over RED HILL.

"We then set about dealing with each weapon pit and bunker in turn. They could be easily distinguished at a range of about 150 yds. Each weapon pit looked just like a small black hole with a hint of disturbed earth round it. There was one bunker on the top of the hill and this was very obvious so we knocked it about good and proper. There was also a bunker in the saddle immediately below us. It was later discovered that there was an anti-tank gun in this bunker. It was facing South, so the Japs had obviously not expected us to come by the route we did. This gun had previously been knocked out by artillery fire.

"All indication of targets was given to the 75 mm gunner by a short burst of Browning and one round HE from the 37 mm gun.* We could thus engage another target whilst the 75 mm dealt with the last one indicated. After we had fired about 25 rounds of 75 mm HE at the weapon pits, our infantry, approaching round the left flank, had got within 50 yds of the enemy positions. One red Verey light was fired and the infantry went in.

"They got held up at once and went to ground, but I could see a weapon pit on the left that I had not previously noticed. One Gurkha Bren gunner fired a burst at it and I gave it some Browning. After this, the Gurkhas appeared to get on to the PIMPLE without difficulty. I then switched my fire on to SECOND PIMPLE and on the village South-East of the PIMPLE, where I saw some Nips running away. Up to date the Gurkhas had had very few casualties.

"Shortly after this, my 75 mm loader had got a hit on the head and was slightly concussed. A 75 mm round jammed in the barrel and the breech block stuck. The Gurkhas were now beginning to consolidate, and, since I was outside the perimeter and the 75 mm gun was definitely out of action, I decided to try and reverse back on to RED HILL. This however proved impossible owing to the soft earth thrown out of the slit trenches and the steepness of the slope—about 35 degrees.

"We then discovered to our horror that immediately the steering sticks were let loose, the tank started slipping down the hill. There was only one thing for it. I ordered the crew to prepare to abandon tank. The guns and wireless were made useless, and then after that I had taken over from the driver, the crew left by the escape hatch. I viewed tremulously the aspect in front of me. I could either let go of the sticks and try to jump out, or attempt to steer it to the bottom. The engine could not be started because immediately the clutch was slipped the tank again moved forward. I decided to steer the tank to the bottom.

"By this time I had quite forgotten my Guardian Angel but he had not forgotten me, for I had not gone 10 yds when the tank stopped on a not quite so steep place and against a small ridge in the ground. Thankfully, I dropped through the escape hatch, and, running faster than I thought I was capable, I reached safety behind RED HILL where the rest of the crew were waiting for me.

"The next day after the enemy in the area had all been liquidated, a party of engineers were taken up to the tank, and a ramp was prepared in front of it to hold it on the slope when it was taken out of gear. When this work was finished, the tank was started up, reversed up RED HILL and driven back by the route it had come. In conclusion I would like to say that but for the splendid work done by the engineers, no tanks could have taken part in this action."

* The tanks must have been either Grants or Lees.

The United States Marine Corps had had an early interest in tanks, establishing an experimental tank platoon in 1923, which took part in manoeuvres and was deployed for garrison duty in China before being disbanded five years later due to budget cuts. In the 1930s, the USMC began to invest in modern light tanks in order to provide their amphibious landing forces with mobility and firepower. By the time the Japanese attack on Pearl Harbor provoked America's entry into the war, the expansion of the tank force was well underway and the first Marine tank unit was deployed to the Pacific in early 1942. In the Pacific there were no large tank-on-tank battles, instead tanks provided critical close support for Marine riflemen.

This is the after-action report for the first few days of the campaign on the island of Iwo Jima, which began on 19 February 1945. While some of the problems, such as those caused by soft beaches and volcanic ash, faced by the tankers were unique to this theatre, others would have been all too familiar to their Army counterparts in Europe. The report notes that 'Due to the rugged terrain encountered on Iwo, orthodox infantry–tank tactics had to be abandoned. Tank tactics were improvised, and in many cases basic principles of employment were disregarded. This was never done because of ignorance of fundamentals; it was done because the tactical situation warranted certain calculated risks. Tank units were eager to support the infantry, and they did everything physically and mechanically possible to furnish that support. If it is certain that tank support of infantry and vice versa was less on Iwo than in previous operations, it is equally certain that the terrain encountered made this situation a foregone conclusion. Errors were made by tank units and by the infantry units they were supporting, but these errors were realized at the time, and corrective measures were immediately initiated. Some tactical errors were easily traceable to the loss of so many key personnel in both the RCTs and the Tank Battalion.'

Iwo Jima: 4th Tank Battalion Report: Narrative

Dog Day: Previously planned arrangements failed, wherein Company "B" of (Second Armored Amphibian Tractor Battalion) would pass beach information to Company "C" of this organization and Company "A", Second Armored Amphibian Tractor Battalion would give information to Company "A". Company "A" received word that the area 200 yards inland and South of Beach Blue One was mined. Company "C", beach reconnaissance units reported Yellow Beaches too soft for landing of tanks and beach exits mined and blocked by shell craters. These units advised that the landing of tanks on Yellow Beaches be delayed until suitable beaching areas and exit routes could be found. The LSMs carrying Company "A" vehicles beached in exactly the opposite order from the plan; this caused confusion and made it necessary for tank platoons to cross over in order to support the BLTs to which they were assigned. The tanks landed under a hail of artillery, mortar and anti-tank fire; all three LSMs were hit and damaged. The Company "A" dozer cut a road through the first terrace inland from Beach Blue One, but hit a large horn mine and received three large calibre direct mortar hits. The dozer was completely destroyed. Company "A" tanks proceeded inland in a column picking their way through shell craters. They encountered a mine field 100 yards inland and were immobilized. The Company "A" tanks fired into the cliff vicinity TA 165 D and E, 166 A and B and 183 U, V, W, and X, and into pill boxes in rear of Blue Beaches. At How plus five (5) hours the First, Third, and Fourth Platoons of Company "B" landed on Beach Blue One to reinforce Company "A"; two Headquarters tanks of Company "B" and the Company "A" retriever landed with this group. Intense artillery and mortar fire continued all day and by How plus seven (7) hours, seven Company "A" tanks were bogged down and five (5) had been knocked out. One Company "B" tank was stuck in a shell hole, and one was hit by 47 mm AT fire and burned. At How plus seven (7) hours the Commanding Officer, Executive Officer and First Platoon Leader of Company "A" were wounded and evacuated and the Commanding Officer of Company "B" assumed command of all tanks in the zone of action of RCT 25. Tanks in this RCT zone bivouacked in an area 25 to 100 yards in rear of the front lines. By nightfall Company "A" had sustained thirty (30) casualties. On the Yellow Beaches the tank of Company "C" had great difficulty due to the loose volcanic ash which immobilized many vehicles and restricted the movement of others. LSM 216 beached at its assigned point on the right flank of Yellow Two, and the first tank off bogged down less than five feet from the ramp's end, blocking the remaining tanks in that vessel. LSM 216 retracted and beached again about 200 yards south where foot reconnaissance showed that tanks would also bog down. The LSM in the meantime had broached on the beach, and it took thirty (30) minutes for it to retract the second time. At 1245 LSM 216 beached on Yellow One, but the sand was too soft, so it withdrew for the third time, and at 1300 beached again discharging its remaining vehicles. LSMs 126 and 211 beached at their assigned spots and were able to discharge their vehicles with little difficulty. Three tanks from LSM 126 struck mines less than 150 yards from the beach, and the remaining three moved to the support of BLT 1/23 finally reaching the No. 1 Airfield just south of the East–West runway turning apron. The tanks from LSM 211 working slowly among mines and shell holes reached the airfield at about noon. The flail which was on this LSM bogged down in soft sand just off the beach. The tanks from LSM 216 also finally made their way to the Airfield knocking out several pillboxes with the CB MK 1 flame thrower. No tanks were able to operate in the zone of BLT 2/23 due to soft sand though several efforts were made to get vehicles into that zone. Eleven (11) tanks and two (2) flame throwing tanks from Company "C" operated with BLT 1/23 until dark when they took up positions in hull defilade just off the edge of the airfield in TA 164 X and Y. LSM 59, carrying the Second Platoon of Company "B", the Company "B" dozer and the Battalion Commander tank, was ordered to beach on Yellow One to reinforce Company "C" at 1400. This LSM was forced to withdraw due to mortar fire after discharging only two vehicles, one of which bogged down on the beach. The other vehicle joined Company "C".

Dog Day Plus One Day: The Commanding Officer of Company "B" who had assumed command of all tanks in the zone of RCT 25 was wounded and evacuated early in the morning, and the Bn-3 was ordered ashore to assume command of Company "B". At the same time the Assistant Bn-3 was ordered ashore to take command of Company "A" and the Battalion Reconnaissance and Liaison Officer to be Executive Officer of Company "A". These officers reached the beach at about noon. Company "A" spent most of the day reorganizing and retrieving damaged and bogged down vehicles, and had eight operative vehicles by dark. Eight (8) tanks from Company "B" supported RCT 25 firing on targets of opportunity. Company "C"'s eleven (11) operational vehicles were divided into three (3) platoons which led the assault companies of RCT 23 across Airfield No. 1. These vehicles could not negotiate the bluff on the NW side of the airfield, and attempts to advance up the taxiways toward Airfield No. 2 were stopped by mines in TA 165 S and 181 X. Three Company "C" vehicles were knocked out, two by mines and one by heavy mortar fire. The remaining vehicles from BSM 59 landed and joined Company "C" at nightfall.

Dog Plus Two Days: Companies "A" and "B" supported RCT 25 with all operational vehicles firing into the cliffs to the front and destroying pill boxes and caves. Two (2) Company "B" vehicles were knocked out by 47 mm AT fire and two threw tracks. These companies bivouacked in TA 165 for the night. Twelve (12) vehicles of Company "C" supported the attack of RCT 23 and reached the high ground across from Airfield No. 1 via the road running from CR 230 through TA 181 Y after this road was cleared of mines. The dozer tank pushed a road to the ridge in TA 182 K where it was knocked out by 47 mm AT fire. The Battalion Maintenance Officer landed with nine (9) mechanics to survey the damage and to aid the Companies in maintenance work. The Assistant Platoon Leader of the Tank Ordnance Platoon also landed with nine (9) enlisted men to aid the Battalion Maintenance Officer.

Dog Plus Three Days: Companies "A" and "B" supported the attack of RCT 25, but were limited by cliffs and rough terrain. One section of tanks cleared some enemy troops from the area adjacent to the East Boat Basin. Company "C" was attached to RCT 21, and operated in the same area as preceding day. Two (2) tanks were knocked out by 47 mm AT fire.

CHAPTER 5: IN THE TURRET

As tank commanders and their crews all discovered, all the training in the world is no substitute for the real thing. British crews landing in Normandy in June 1944 had spent years training in England, but now they came up against German troops with years of battle experience behind them.

The following narrative of part of the battle for Raamsdonk (31 October 1944) was based on a report from 21 Army Group, and was published in *Current Reports from Overseas* 82 (28 March 1945). As the advance was ongoing, it does not identify the Yeomanry tank squadron and the Highland infantry platoon involved. The Kangaroo was a tank chassis converted into an armoured personnel carrier.

A Tank Troop in Action

Introduction

This report of an action by a troop of Sherman tanks and an infantry platoon affords a good example of quick thinking and initiative on the part of individual tank commanders. The country was such that tanks could only operate along roads, and the flat open fields yielded no cover for infantry.

The plan

During the operations designed to clear the enemy from the south bank of the River Maas, a battalion of a Highland regiment, supported by one squadron of a Yeomanry tank regiment, were to advance through our forward positions in the area of Raamsdonk, with the task of seizing the bridge at Geertruidenburg, thereby cutting the enemy's escape route to the north.

The enemy were known to hold the stretch of road north from Raamsdonk with machine guns and infantry anti-tank weapons, and unconfirmed reports stated that one Mark IV tank was also located in this area. An attack by tanks and dismounted infantry the previous day had proved unsuccessful and two tanks had been destroyed by enemy Bazookas.

It was decided to push a troop of tanks, and one platoon of the Highland battalion mounted in two Kangaroos, through and on to Laan by the road that turned west near the church, relying on speed and armour to overcome the opposition. If this project was successful a second troop, leading the rest of the company – also mounted in Kangaroos – was to follow in their wake, leaving the mopping up to the remaining, dismounted companies. On arrival at Laan the leading company was to dismount and push on towards Geertruidenburg, supported by a troop of tanks. The other companies would follow up after the completion of mopping up operations in the Raamsdonk area.

Execution of the plan

At 1600 hours, after ten minutes' shelling of the road leading to the church, the troop of tanks and platoon of infantry set off. The order of march was Serjeant 'T' (75 millimetre gun tank), Lieutenant 'M' (75 millimetre gun tank), the two Kangaroos, Corporal 'P' (75 millimetre gun tank), and Corporal 'G' (17 pounder gun tank).

The column advanced at a good speed, firing into the houses on either side of the road, and were approaching the Red House at H plus 10, when the artillery concentrations, which had been directed on to the area of the church, lifted. On reaching the Red House Serjeant 'T' fired one round of HE at the White House, and a vivid green flash followed by flame and smoke, testified both to the accuracy of aim and to the happy thought that had inspired the shooting. By this time SP Gun No. 1 had suddenly appeared on the left hand side of the road south of the church, having probably moved out from the White House area. Serjeant 'T' himself did not see it, due to the smoke, but his gunner – Trooper 'D' – spotted it and promptly put three AP rounds six inches apart into the front centre, thereby putting the SP gun out of action. The driver – Trooper 'O' – kept going and just managed to squeeze past this obstacle, but rounding the bend opposite the church, he swerved to avoid some rubble and the right hand bank gave way, with the result that the tank dropped four feet into a ditch, at an angle of 30 degrees. It was then that Serjeant 'T' spotted SP Gun No. 2 through the smoke; the gunner traversed and brewed it up with the first shot from their position in the ditch. So far, owing to quick and accurate shooting, two SP guns had been knocked out before either had been able to fire a shot.

Meanwhile, Lieutenant 'M' passed SP Gun No. 1, and probably due to the smoke, had the misfortune to ditch himself. The Kangaroo that followed,

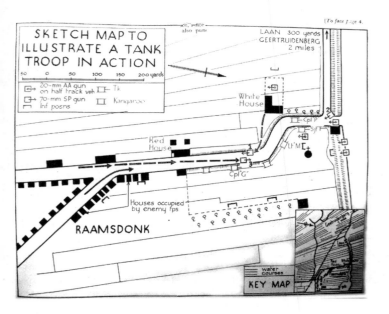

[To face page 4.

SKETCH MAP TO
ILLUSTRATE A TANK
TROOP IN ACTION

under legitimate misapprehension that the SP gun was still in action, most gallantly charged it, lost a right hand sprocket in the process, skidded and also ended up in the ditch. The commander of the second Kangaroo, to whom the situation appeared far from clear, gave the order to halt.

The advance had now come to a standstill and the infantry platoon dismounted from the two Kangaroos and reorganized in the area in the church.

It was then that Serjeant 'T' got through to the squadron commander on the wireless and, considering the circumstances, gave a clear picture of what was happening, and so enabled the commanding officer of the infantry battalion to size up the situation and to despatch a second troop of tanks and platoon of infantry round by the southern road to Laan. Serjeant 'T' also rang up Corporal 'P' and ordered him to try and come up past the obstacles in order to give protection on the front and left flank. Corporal 'P' duly succeeded and took up a position near Serjeant 'T' from where he shot three 20 millimetre anti-aircraft guns mounted on half tracked vehicles and compelled the enemy infantry, who were firing their Spandaus and rifles at the ditched tanks, to run for cover. Later, by patrolling up and down the road, he scotched all enemy attempts to approach and destroy the tanks and Kangaroos.

Corporal 'G', for his part, had attempted to follow Corporal 'P', but since his tank was the fifth vehicle to swing round SP Gun No. 1, the bank had become so loosened that it gave way and he was ditched.

Lieutenant 'M' dismounted from his tank to try and contact the platoon commander in the area of the church and was killed by Spandau fire.

By this time SP Gun No. 3 had approached from Raamsdonk with the object of taking the column in rear. It dealt faithfully with the second Kangaroo and, believing Corporal 'G' to be out of action, drove up and ground to a standstill immediately in front of his ditched tank. Corporal 'G''s gunner was just able to traverse the necessary few inches to get on, but even then could only see the top six inches of the target owing to the steep angle at which his tank rested in the ditch. But he let fly with a round of HE and the SP gun straightway burst into flames. At the same time Corporal 'P' spotted this SP gun through the smoke and put two rounds of AP into it from the opposite direction.

During the whole period covered by this operation, the column was subjected to heavy shelling and fired at from all directions by Spandaus. The crews of the ditched tanks remained inside and used Sten guns and grenades as opportunities appeared. The White House, three SP guns, and two Kangaroos were on fire, and the whole area was wreathed in smoke. Some time later Lieutenant 'M''s tank caught fire and added to the conflagration, and the crew baled out and joined forces with the infantry platoon. At the same time Serjeant 'T' shouted across to the platoon commander and told him that the bulk of the battalion were going round by a different route and that the platoon was to hold on until dark and then to rejoin the battalion as best it could. He also communicated with Corporal 'P', kept the situation under control, and found time to send back information. The squadron commander also talked direct to Corporal 'P' who gave him a clear picture of the situation.

Two further half-tracks were destroyed and at approximately 1830 hours just as it was getting dark and the shelling and explosions were dying down, orders were given to withdraw.

Reginald James Spittles was a pre-war territorial soldier with the 2nd Northamptonshire Yeomanry. In anticipation of war, he was called up on 1 September 1939. Initially the regiment had just one real tank, but over the next four and a half years Reg and the other men were trained up to become tank crewmen. Reg became a driver, qualifying as a Driver Mechanic Class 2 in 1940. When the regiment finally went into action in June 1944, as an armoured reconnaissance regiment with the 11th Armored Division in Normandy, Reg was the commander of 'Baker' tank in a troop of Cromwells. His years of training, both before and during the war, stood him and his crew – four of them still teenagers – in good stead in the weeks ahead.

In his later years, Reg visited his local college to tell the students stories of his time as a tank commander. Eventually he wrote dozens of these stories down. It is striking how clear and vivid his descriptions are, even though they were written decades after the event. At the end of this account of his first action, he added the note 'You have to imagine the noise, smell, fear and atmosphere of being in a tank in action!' Three of his accounts of his time as a tank commander in 1944 serve as a fitting postscript.

Baptism of Fire

I was the Troop Corporal of No. 2 'A' Squadron, 2nd Northants Yeomanry.

This is my account of my first day in 'Fighting Combat', I had been called-up for War Service on Sept 1st 1939 aged 21 years, it was after 4 years plus that during the night of June 16th 1944 that with my Squadron we landed on 'Juno Beach' at the village of 'Courselles', we moved inland and eventually we settled among the orchards close to 'Cruelly', we were to stay there until June 25th.

During the night (June 25th) 'A' Squadron were moved forward to our Forward Holding Positions and by 0300 hours we were settled in position.

As the dawn approached and it started to get light we were suddenly awakened by a most terrific bang, the vibration shook the tank (Cromwell, 35 tons in weight), you do not sleep in a tank but this brought us back to life anyway.

It appeared we were sitting in amongst a Battery of 25 pound Artillery Guns, the firing lasted about an hour which we endured all flaps closed down and a blanket wrapped around our heads! It appeared this was part of the preliminary bombardment on the town (village) of Cheux which the 15 Scottish Infantry Division were to attack and occupy.

After they had occupied the town we (A Squadron) were to proceed through the town and the next village of Haut-Du-Bosch and proceed to the River Odon where were located 3 bridges, we were to occupy each bridge by placing one troop on each with the other two troops in between (there are 5 troops to each squadron), make a report by radio of conditions, this would be followed by a squadron of tanks with infantry from the 23rd Hussars to support us to be followed up by a build-up of more troops.

All very simple and jolly!

In Yorkshire, UK, simple! In Normandy, YUK!

In training towns and villages were complete, in Normandy they were just heaps of rubble after being shelled and fought over, it took 'A' Squadron 1½ hours to go through. Our first casualty was our 2nd in command Captain Wyvell Raynsford, shot through the head by a supposed sniper.

It appeared to me the town was still occupied by as many Germans as there were Scotchmen.

They were trying to climb on the tank, put sticky bombs on the sides, tossing grenades at the turrets, shooting at tank commanders, our Sten Guns came in very handy.

Whenever we became completely stationary I found the best solution to keep them from coming too close was to throw out around us phosphorus grenades. Phosphorus burns human flesh while it is in contact with the air, I suppose today it would be banned from use, it was the only time in any fighting I was involved in that I had to use them but it was a case of survival, at least it was to me – I was too young to die yet!

But of course we did eventually get through – I had assumed we would stay on the road and just motor down to the river and deal with any obstacle we met on the way. We motored through Haut-Du-Bosch (No shelling! No trouble!) but then our Squadron Leader Major Bobby Peel started to set the squadron out in what I would call a Battle Formation. This brought us to a stop while each troop took up position. My troop No. 2 were in reserve so were just sitting there watching all this happening.

No. 4 Troop 'Lt Stock' was on the road on our left flank, he just kept on motoring and carried on down to the river, No. 1 and HQ Troop had come to stop apparently because of a deep ditch. No. 3 Troop 'Lt Lowenger' on the right flank was motoring (about 25 to 30 mph) away up on a long gradual slope to an horizon of bushes and trees. (He was in a cornfield.)

This was the sort of speed we would have used in an exercise in England where if you made an error of judgement you would not get killed or injured, I remarked to my wireless operator about it who casually said 'Soft Sod'. I agreed. I looked away in other directions before looking back to 3 Troop where to my amazement 2 of the Cromwells were on fire (brewing up). I had never seen a tank on fire before and here was two out of three burning furiously, I just thought 'Bloody Hell'.

The next shock was to hear Bobby Peel on the radio saying 'You see what's happened, get up there!' My Troop Leader Lt Hobson said 'Hello Baker (my codename). Take the lead away you go!' I said to my driver 'Advance and we'll go in between those two burning Cromwells for a bit of cover. Take your time 15 will do!'

Lt Hobson who was always full of 'go-go' on exercises came on the B Set radio (used for the three tanks in a troop without interference from other users) and said 'Hello Baker get a move on.' I chose to ignore his request and so eventually arrived between the two burning Cromwells.

From this position I could see virtually nothing, so moving forward slowly until I could begin to see farther over the crest and into the ground beyond, eventually I could see the whole valley before me where to my amazement I could see the equivalent number of Mk-4 tanks the size of a squadron 'About 20' plus a few Panthers, they were at quite a good speed from 'Left to Right' obviously moving from one position to another. I reported what I could see to my Troop Leader who informed the 'Major' who promptly said 'SHOOT THE BLOODY THINGS!' For as long as they remained in our view we did, knocking out several before they eventually disappeared.

The weather that day was terrible, on and off heavy rain showers with thunder and lightning, it created a slight ground mist (we had been having warm weather so the ground was warm). This made it difficult to see ground targets and created a fear of enemy infantry infiltration as we had no infantry support of our own.

At about 1700hrs we were ordered to withdraw to our start point, it appeared that No. 4 Troop had reached the river and given a report and were now on their way back. The expected follow-up forward operation to the river had been cancelled so we withdrew with No. 1 Troop Lt Sharpe taking the lead, HQ Troop to follow and then No. 2 Troop.

We began to withdraw with Lt Hobson in the lead followed by Troop Sgt Jack Mann and finally 'BAKER', we had our turret facing to the rear as per drill when suddenly a figure stood up in the corn waving his arms. Looking through my binoculars I could see it was Sgt Albert Coulson, we stopped and on the B Set I informed Lt Hobson we intended to return to collect him, and we hoped his crew. I received no reply. After an interval Sgt Mann camp up and said he would wait until he saw our return.

On our arrival we found Sgt Coulson's driver had been killed with Sgt Coulson and two of his crew quite badly wounded but Trooper Hipkin not injured, so with Trooper Hipkin to help me we put all four of them on the back of our tank. Cromwell tanks are well suited for carrying people on the back being very flat, we now started our journey back.

Sgt Mann disappeared in the town rubble and we followed. As we approached the far side I saw a track leading out of the debris along the side of a high wall and directed my driver to follow up the track, unfortunately as we approached, the tank, slipping and sliding on the loose bricks etc, lurched to one side and became jammed. The engine stalled with the tank stuck in gear, we would need a push up the back to relieve the pressure to slip into neutral gear but my more pressing problem was the 3 wounded men on the back plus Hipkin.

Fortunately a troop of 4 Bren Gun Carriers came down the track and one of these took our 4 men away to the rear for treatment. Having reported our situation and location I had expected our squadron recovery tank to come to our assistance. But no, someone had the bright idea to inform No. 4 Troop to oblige on their way back from the river.

Spasmodic firing was still going on so apart from my own turret flaps being slightly open we were completely shut down, giving directions to No. 4 Troop of our position on the radio.

Eventually they arrived. Sgt Reg King decided to give us the push, now I had to sit on the front of his tank holding a block of wood (we carried 2 for just such an occasion) while the driver eased his tank slowly forward to give me time to position the block in the correct position to take the push. The push duly delivered we were free (back on the road).

We now rejoined the squadron, cleared our turret of empty shell cases. I went off to make my report to find Lt Hobson (on behalf of the troop?) was credited with the rescue of Sgt Albert Coulson's crew.

I claimed we had destroyed one Mk-4 German tank and one large half-track infantry carrier after machine gunning the occupants, also engaging enemy fire from ground troops, using machine gun, HE and smoke shell.

We also had the sad task of burying our 2nd i.c. Captain Wyvell Raynsford who had been killed on our approach to our first action, this was very upsetting for Major Bobby Peel who had known him and the family for many years and was well liked and respected by all of the lower ranks.

The driver of Sgt Coulson's tank who was killed was Tpr Charlie Haman. I have no knowledge of the Corporal or his crew of 3 Troop other than they were not reported as casualties so must assume they lived to fight another day.

Reg was wounded on 19 July, during Operation *Goodwood*, and re-joined his troop ten days later. He had a new tank and a new driver. The new driver was the cause of no small trouble when he burnt out the engine valves, causing the engine to seize up on the battlefield during a fighting withdrawal on 4 August. Reg and his crew returned safely, walking the 5 miles back to safety in the dark, but the regiment was not so lucky, only 14 tanks returned of the 65! By 12 August the regiment had been rebuilt and continued to liberate towns. One month after landing in Normandy 2nd Northants Yeomanry was disbanded.

The Night it all Went Wrong

We were a troop of four Cromwells from the 2nd Northants Yeomanry. I was the troop corporal with two sergeants and a lieutenant troop officer. After 2NY was disbanded we were now with B Sqn of the 1st RTR having joined them on August 20th 1944.

By the 2nd–3rd September 1944 we were operating in the area of the Lille Coalfields, an area of railways, canals and narrow roads. The circumstances for tank commanders were very awkward because we had 'run off' our maps and Troop Leaders were relying on information from the Squadron Leader who was usually relying on the local Maquis for his information and most likely on the local school map.

On this occasion we were in one of the small towns of the Coalfields and our troop was instructed to proceed down through the town marketplace and to locate a bridge and defend it until such time that the Squadron could organise a stronger force to follow on to secure the area. This was all during the night and in total darkness.

Our Troop Leader came back from his meeting with the Squadron Leader. Thinking it would be quicker, he briefly outlined the intention and said follow me. We went down to a T junction (here we made our error) and turned left instead of right and suddenly found out we were out in the countryside instead of the market place. We came to a turning off to our right (quick natter on the B set) and decided we could take this right turn and approach the bridge from that side of the town (it did not appear to be a very large town). Having taken this turn we then came to a 'T' junction and turned right.

We passed a very large house on our right in its own grounds (a country hall) and came to a railway station and pulled into the station yard, we four Cromwells making enough noise to wake everybody. We four commanders decided that not having a clue of our position decided to return to the town and carry on with the original plan through the market place. So off we went, Troop Officer in the lead and I was the third tank in line.

Suddenly just as we came to the large house the road was full of German transport lorries that were pulling out to form a convoy facing towards the town. With no way past, a deep ditch on each side of the road, suddenly a German officer with a torch halted a lorry halfway out of the gateway for us to proceed (you must note we were closed down except for the commander) giving our Troop Leader a very impressive Nazi salute he waved us on.

Now as soon as my driver heard the word 'Jerries' he slammed his visor shut, now there is no way you can see anything through a periscope in the dark! So with him trying to keep up with the tank in front, I was having to do my best by telling him 'left tiller' or 'right tiller' to keep him from going into the dyke on either side of the road. When we came to the left turn to continue our return we had to stop and using the pick head managed to prise open his jammed visor; with me calling him all the stupid B******s could think of). The fourth tank caught up with us and pulled in behind, the commander was also bollocking his driver who had decided on his own initiative to side swipe the last lorry into the dyke, thinking it a bit of fun!

We then carried on to catch up with the other two who had gone on. We caught up with them all right! The second (sergeant's) tank driver had clipped a large stone wall on the corner of the second turn left and broken a track which had run off. So what do we do? It would take too long to do a repair so we put a towrope for the Troop Leader to tow the tank and I towed the track behind us, swinging from left to right creating a shower of sparks every time it hit a kerb or other stone object with the fourth tank behind us being the only free running tank bringing up the rear.

Anyway we returned to our starting point, having done no more than let every 'Jerry' in the town know we had arrived! 'B' Squadron, 1st RTR – what a way to arrive?!

After our Troop Leader had reported to the Squadron Leader, it was decided we would go back to do it right (second time around), our disabled Cromwell was replaced with a 17-pounder Sherman, so once more we went down into the town. Our Troop Leader in the front, followed by the Troop sergeant with me behind him and the Sherman behind me. We came to a 'T' junction. Round the corner goes 'Sun-ray' followed by 'Able', I was half way round when suddenly everywhere became bright as day. Jerry was putting up star shells on top of the houses and what appeared to be a multiple 20mm gun of some sort started firing at the first two tanks. Talk about fireworks! Bits were flying off the two Cromwells which both started to reverse. I started to reverse but having to use our tillers to turn the corner, the Sergeant's tank was catching us up so I thought it would be quicker to do a neutral turn around which I told my driver to do. Round we came and without stopping, straightened up and went straight into the front of the Sherman and then did his best to try and shove the 17-pounder out of the turret. What the 17-pounder gunner thought I hate to think! All the fittings which these old Desert Rats always put on their tanks were being ripped off and finally I managed to convince my driver to slip into neutral and roll back off.

Why I'll never know but nothing happened by way of an inquiry ever came of it. So maybe we didn't do as much damage as it appeared. Anyway the war carried on and when daylight came the REME came to repair the damaged tank and we became heroes to the local population and became our normal efficient four Cromwell Tank Troop helping to win the war!

The advance continued, through Belgium and into Holland. While checking the tank's gun after maintenance – made particularly necessary by constant firing in the very heavy fighting that the squadron experienced while in support of American troops during Operation *Market Garden* – Reg unknowingly loaded a faulty shell into the gun, which almost immediately fired. The shell injured an officer, and Reg was hauled up in front of a court of enquiry before it was decided that there was no case to answer as it was purely a fault in manufacture. However, Reg would be indirectly punished for his bad luck shortly afterwards.

My almost decoration

The Regiment (1st RTR) was once more advancing across open country. One of our final objectives was the very important town of Hertogenbosch, not all that large but a cross section of road and rail and canal, a most important combination and very vital to the Germans' transport communication network.

The leading tank of the leading troop of our squadron had been knocked out by enemy action and I had been sent forward to take his place. The nomal formation was that, slightly forward of the tank in the dykes which were dry but about 7 to 8 feet deep (approx 2½ metres) each side of the road would be a section (approx 6–7 men) of the infantry to flush out any enemy troops. On the second day we came to a situation where the enemy had felled a very large tree across the road at a point where there was what appeared to be a very large farm with several cottages and outbuildings, behind this there also was a wooded area, the enemy had chosen a very ideal place to create a strong point.

I would point out that our tank was a Cromwell, 35 ton in weight, with a 75 mm main weapon plus two Besa machine guns, with a crew of five men and a further assortment of weapons.

I had stopped about 400 yards (metres) short of the farm and through my binoculars could see no sign of enemy troops. The next thing would be for the infantry to send a patrol to the area, it could be that there was no one there. As a preliminary to this we fired several HE shells and smoke shells into the area, this was replied by heavy machine gun fire, so there was someone there. To me it seemed obvious they did not have a weapon of any sort to deal with a tank at 400 yards – anti-tank gun or another tank.

The hatch that the commander and the gunner use to get in and out of the tank consisted of a circular smaller turret known as a cupola which could be used to traverse independently of the main turret, the top being two separate halves. On the turret top behind the small cupola I had two small sacks of earth so my head was actually in a three-sided box to give some protection from a sniper. From this position I could observe all the traffic on the main road going in and out of the town, now my troubles were about to start!

It seems the local infantry were having a bad time so no-one could be spared to mount a patrol to flush out the strong point, added to this the enemy were now firing what was known as air bursts. These were HE shells which were timed to explode in the air, which meant every time this happened you received a shower of shrapnel (metal fragments). For me I just closed my turret flaps down and then popped up afterwards. Unfortunately the two sections of infantry in the dykes were becoming casualties so they were withdrawn leaving me in complete isolation, my protection had gone! Strange as it may seem there are times a tank needs protecting from enemy infiltration. I was in need as you will see!

I requested permission to pull back to a safer area but as it appeared I was the only tank in a good position to observe the forward area I was told to stay put and keep reporting my observations. Now that the dykes were empty the enemy could now approach me unseen as I could not see down into them and the following disaster happened. During our time in England training my wireless operator and myself had developed a method whereby if I wished to speak to him while he was shut down (he had his own entry flaps in the turret) to save time and not have to lower myself down into the turret I would reach across and rap on his flaps with my knuckles he would 'pop up' like a Jack in a box to see what I wanted. Unfortunately an enterprising German came along the dyke on my operator's side and proceeded to shower me with hand grenades, unfortunately my operator heard them bouncing on the turret and thinking it was me 'popped up'. Result! Several grenades hit his shoulders and dropped into the tank.

My immediate reaction was to shout for everyone to bail out into the left-hand dyke, this we proceeded to do but not before the hand grenades exploded. I had to wait behind the turret to make sure my gunner was getting out all right, he couldn't get out until I had gone. Having seen he was coping I jumped down into the dyke and started to check who was there and to what extent injuries they had received. I myself had received shrapnel to my right leg, my operator to his legs and back, my driver was in a total state of shock because he thought he was blinded. He had a piece of shrapnel in his forehead and the blood had filled his eye and face, my co-driver was the only one not injured, my gunner appeared not to have arrived. So I told my co-driver to give me a lift up and saw my gunner lying on the road behind the tank, I climbed out and dragged him into the dyke. There seemed to be a lot of blood around his neck and shoulders, not realising but the Germans had been firing at us with a small arms and my gunner had been hit in the shoulder just as he was about to jump down and knocked himself out when he hit the ground. I now had to organise to get us all to the first aid post. I put my operator and driver together to help each other and my co-driver and myself (painfully) carried my unconscious gunner between us, that way we duly arrived for dressings.

After we had all been attended to the Sergeant Major proceeded to take down my details of what happened, while he was doing this the first aid post was cleared of casualties including my crew, leaving my co-driver and myself behind. I suggested to the Sergeant Major we should recover the tank before the Germans got round to throwing a petrol bomb into it and set it on fire. I suggested if my co-driver came with me to bunk me up from the dyke I would get in to see if it was still working. I could then drive it back. We did this but no luck, it didn't work, the only other thing was to tow it back using another tank.

Using the 17 pounder Sherman my co-driver and myself returned to our tank and fixed the tow cable, my co-driver got in to operate the steering tillers. I told him which one to operate to keep the tank straight and not go into the dyke on either side, this way we were able to effect a recovery, afterwards being told how lucky we had been because the Germans had been taking pot shots at us!

By now the REME had arrived, unfortunately in a (white) half-track not the normal recovery tank to tow our tank away. After an inspection they were able to fix a wire and able to start the engine but on the understanding that the engine should not be switched off until we reached our destination, this was to be our Regimental 'B' (Base) Echelon where the REME intended to re-wire the tank – the grenades had destroyed all our fuse boxes and wiring, this would take about six days. My co-driver thought because I was a driver mechanic by trade it would be better for me to drive, he was frightened he might stall the engine, so I had a second morphine injection for the pain in my right leg, which I would have to use on the accelerator pedal all the way back, a distance of 10 to 15 miles, so with the map on my lap, we set off and in due course we arrived safely.

My co-driver's name was Bill Barnett, so Bill and myself fixed a small tent using the canvas sheet from the tank for a temporary home, I would be attending to our medical Officer twice a day (morning and evening) for my wounds (mainly my right leg). It was on the third day our Sergeant Major arrived in his Jeep to take me to Brigade Headquarters, he said you're going to be pleasantly surprised!

On arrival I was invited to enter the brigadier's caravan (higher-ranking officers all had a caravan) I saluted and was invited to sit down (my bad leg). The Brigadier then read to me the Sergeant Major's report of the action "recovering the tank under fire" and my conduct in getting my crew back under a difficult situation, he said I had acted in the best traditions of the Tank Regiment.

He then went on to inform me that the officer who had been injured with my premature shell wasn't too badly injured and would eventually return to the regiment, he then went on to say, although there is no punishment involved because it was an accident, he himself thought there should be some sort of retribution! So he suggested that if he was to destroy the Sergeant Major's report and recommendation, all parties would be satisfied (who was I to argue!).

So with his promise of "good hunting in Germany" I was dismissed. On the return journey the Sergeant Major asked what he was putting me in for (decoration) after I told him he said a word that suggested the Brigadier was born out of wedlock.

To finish off, it seemed my wounds were becoming too bad for our medical officer to deal with in the short-term so I was sent to No. 8 British Field Hospital in Belgium. I was duly downgraded to C1 which meant I could not serve with a fighting unit.

Sources

Introduction

'Tank Gunnery', *Notes from Theatres of War 14: Western Desert and Cyrenaica, August/December, 1942* (War Office, 1943), accessed National Archives, WO 208/3108

1 Royal Tank Regiment Lessons (1943), accessed Tank Museum, Bovington

Chapter 1: Crew Training

'Royal Armoured Corps', *Notes from Theatres of War 13: North Africa—Algeria and Tunisia, November 1942–March 1943* (War Office, 1943), accessed National Archives, WO 208/3108

Military Training Pamphlet No. 51: Troop Training for Cruiser Tank Troops (The War Office, 1941), accessed National Archives, WO 231/126.

Instruction Book, Infantry Tanks, Matilda Mks I, II, III, IV, V, accessed Tank Museum, Bovington

FM 17-5: Armored Force Field Manual: Armored Force Drill (War Department, 18 January 1943)

'Operating the Panzer IV', *Intelligence Bulletin* Vol. 1, No. 4 (Military Intelligence Service, War Department, December 1942)

Infantry Tank Mark II, IIA and IIA* (1941 edition), accessed Tank Museum, Bovington

Tank Driver's Handbook, Light Tank M-2 (1941), accessed Tank Museum, Bovington

Training Notes from Recent Fighting in Tunisia (G-3 Training Section AFHQ, 1943)

Part II, B Fire Orders, Directive No. 1 (3rd Royal Tank Regiment), accessed Tank Museum, Bovington

P. Kolomeisev, 'Training to Shoot from an Moving Tank', *Tank Journal* (1939), translated by Tobie Matthew

Chapter 2: Tactics

FM 17-30 *Armored Force Field Manual: Tank Platoon* (War Department, 22 October 1942)

Military Training Pamphlet No. 22, Part III: Tactical Handling of Army Tank Battalions—Employment (The War Office, 1939), accessed National Archives, WO 231/128

Extract from General Friedrich Cochenhausen, *Taktisches Handbuch für den Truppenführer und seinen Gehilfen (Tactical Handbook for the Troop Commander and his Assistants)* (Mittler-Verlag, 13th edition, 1940), translated for the US *Technical and Tactical Trends* 7 (Military Intelligence Service, US War Department, 10 September 1942)

'General Order 14', translated and reproduced in *Notes from Theatres of War* 16: November 1942–1943 (The War Office, 1943) accessed National Archives, WO 208/3108. Another translation was printed in the American *Tactical and Technical Trends* 28 (Military Intelligence Service, US War Department, 1 July 1943).

Chapter 3: In Theatre

Instruction Book Driving and Maintenance. Tanks Infantry Matilda I, II, III, IV, V, accessed Tank Museum, Bovington

T-34 Short Service Manual (Military Press, People's Commissariat of Defence of the USSR, Moscow 1942) accessed Tank Museum, Bovington

'Fatigue of Tank Crews', *Notes from Theatres of War* 10: Cyrenaica and Western Desert, January/June, 1942 (War Office, 1942), accessed National Archives, WO 208/3108

Battle Standing Orders and Training Notes, 1st Royal Tank Regiment, accessed Tank Museum, Bovington

'Russian Tank Camouflage in Winter', translated and published in *Tactical and Technical Trends* 17 (Military Intelligence Service, War Department, 28 January 1943)

'Finnish Tank Traps', Tactical and Technical Trends 21 (Military Intelligence Service, War Department, 25 March 1943)

Chapter 4: Knowing the Enemy

Extracts from 'Russian AFVs – Technical and Tactical', a lecture delivered at German AFV Training School at Wunsdorf, March 1942, translated and reproduced in *Weekly Intelligence Review* No. 14 (GSI GHQ PERSIA AND IRAQ FORCE, 30 December 1942) accessed Tank Museum, Bovington

'Russian tank tactics against German tanks', translated and reproduced in *Tactical and Technical Trends* 16 (Military Intelligence Service, War Department, 14 January 1943)

'Report of the first Tiger I in action', *Technical Intelligence Bulletin* No. 15 (Supreme Headquarters Allied Expeditionary Force, Office of Assistant Chief of Staff, G-2, Main Headquarters, 29 May 1945) accessed Tank Museum, Bovington

'Tiger' versus 'Stalin', *Nachrichtenblatt der Panzertruppen* (September 1944), translated and supplied to the School of Tank Technology, accessed Tank Museum, Bovington

'Tanks in New Guinea', *Notes from Theatres of War* 17: Far East, April–November 1943 (War Office, 1944) accessed National Archives, WO 208/3108

British Military Training Pamphlet 52: Warfare in the Far East (The War Office, December 1944) accessed National Archives, WO 231/126

'The Attack on Red Hill, 28 May 44', *Current Reports from Overseas* 64 (The War Office, 22 November 1944) accessed National Archives, WO 208/3111

Annex Jig to Fourth Martin Division Operations Report: Iwo Jima, 4th Tank Battalion Report (Headquarters, 4th Tank Battalion, 4th Marine Division, 18 April 1945)

Chapter 5: In the Turret

'A Tank Troop in Action', *Current Reports from Overseas* 82 (The War Office, 28 March 1945) accessed National Archives, WO 208/3111

All material by Reginald James Spittles reproduced courtesy of the Tank Museum, Bovington